People-Empathy:

Key to Painless Supervision

People-Empathy:
Key to Painless Supervision

Jack Danner

Parker Publishing Co., Inc.   West Nyack, New York

Library of Congress Cataloging in Publication Data

Danner, Jack
    People-empathy, key to painless supervision.

    1. Supervision of employees. 2. Empathy.
I. Title.
HF5549.D27   658.3'02   76-15290
ISBN 0-13-655738-4

How You Will Gain
By Reading This Book

This book will help you manage better through empathy. Here is what this book can do for you.

Chapter 1 shows you how to recognize achievement, growth, responsibility and recognition as the true motivators. Through them, you will turn your employees on and tune them in. Mastering these four motivators will make supervision painless and will help you turn conflict into a creative tool.

Malcolm P. had three engineers, each working on only a portion of a bridge project with Malcolm doing the final coordination. Malcolm realized that his engineers were becoming bored and restless, but with people-empathy he rotated assignments and his engineers consistently performed at increasingly higher levels with the result that his entire department enjoyed a handsome year-end bonus.

Learn in Chapter 2 how people-empathy obtains results and provides achievement for your employees, while Chapter 3 gives you guidelines for employee growth. You learn to recognize the difference between growth and job enrichment.

This book shows you that job enrichment can lead to growth. You see that when you manage with people-empathy, you know that job enrichment is not to be mistaken for growth itself. You learn that when you provide for growth, the use of people-empathy helps you seek to use job enrichment as one step along the way. You are shown how to recognize that growth comes from more than job enrichment, and the two are not really one and the same.

Although Myron V. was enchanted with job enrichment, it wasn't long before he was pressed to come up with bigger and better things. He began to manage with people-empathy and looked beyond job enrichment to those things that provided growth for his employees. With this new outlook, Myron became a more effective manager and was rewarded with a salary increase of five thousand dollars at year-end.

Chapter 5 helps you become a better manager by developing your employees through increased responsibility. In this chapter you learn how people-empathy calls for you to remove controls and increase accountability.

Chapter 11 provides guidelines for properly administering controls. You see how management by objectives can work for you.

This book also shows you how to provide proper recognition for your employees in Chapter 6. In this chapter you learn how providing recognition helps to improve employee performance. You also learn that recognition is more than superficial praise and applause.

Tom S. noticed that the pilots, flight attendants, ground crews, mechanics, and ticket attendants had no concept of the management organization of their company. He set up a new indoctrination program with people-empathy so that each new employee was introduced to the top management and given a tour of the headquarters to see what made the operations tick. This simple act, done with people-empathy, paid off by providing recognition for the employees of the airline and led to Tom S. being promoted to the position of corporate vice-president.

Chapter 7 helps you when you must implement a change which, in any organization, can be the source of many headaches. Change often creates a crisis situation that detracts from the main objectives of the organization. However, by using this book you see that change *can* be brought about effectively and painlessly through people-empathy.

Joyce was a manager who used people-empathy and did not assume that she knew all the answers necessary to make changes. Calling all her employees together for a meeting, she explained the problems they faced in trying to make an outmoded system keep pace with the city as it grew. Within three weeks they had installed one of the most modern systems of any water works and, as a result of the efficiencies gained by the system, the mayor and board of city commissioners were able to authorize a handsome salary increase as a bonus for Joyce.

Chapter 9 shows you how discipline can be positive and the difference between punishment and discipline, while Chapter 10 provides guidance for dealing with special problems. Emergencies can be handled with ease. Learn how developing rapport with ethnic groups helps make supervision painless. All of these activities, if done with empathy, can make supervision easier and help you become a better manager.

This book helps managers in the effective handling of situations in the business world. As a "how-to" book, it gives a prescription for the way you should approach various problems and shows methods that, through experience, have been found to work. This book will stimulate thought and by showing you these methods, help you develop PEOPLE-EMPATHY: KEY TO PAINLESS SUPERVISION.

                                        Jack Danner

Contents

2

3

4

Guaranteeing Yourself Constant, Reliable Feedback . . .   *71*

5

6

7

How to Gain Employee Support Painlessly When Initiating Needed Change *119*

8

Understanding Employee Needs, Emotions and Personalities Through People-Empathy *137*

9

10

11

1

*Recognizing and Meeting
the Motivational Needs
of Employees*

Much work has been done on the motivation of the workforce. Many books have been written and many people in the management consultant, psychological, and social science fields have given their attention to the motivation of the employee. However, research in this growing field has not been without conflict. Traditionalists maintain that employees are motivated by promises of money or the threat of losing their job, while behavioral scientists tell us that this is not true. The work environment is *expected* by the employee, but what motivates a person is the work itself. The true route to motivation is through people-empathy.

The importance of motivation is apparent in the costs resulting from dissatisfaction in the workforce. A manager need only look at the performance of his workers in such areas as quality, turnover, absenteeism, lateness, failure to meet production standards, and the accident-frequency rate to tell if his employees are motivated and if he is managing with people-empathy. The manager whose employees are motivated can consistently expect to meet or exceed his goals and objectives. The manager who uses empathy can expect to have employees that are motivated.

THE FOUR PRINCIPAL MOTIVATIONAL NEEDS

Behavioral scientists have a general hypothesis that employees will be motivated when certain basic needs are satisfied. These needs are present in varying degrees in different people. The makeup of the person affected determines the amount of each of these needs that is present. The hypothesis basically concludes that without *any* of these needs being satisfied, motivation will not be present. It takes a manager operating with empathy to be able to determine what these needs are and to tell what level of satisfaction has been reached in his employees.

There are four principal needs which, when satisfied, produce motivation:

1. Achievement
2. Recognition
3. Responsibility
4. Growth

Some lists also include the work itself. These needs apply not only to the hourly workers, but to everyone in the organization. When you recognize these needs and what they mean, you are beginning to manage with empathy and are on the road to motivating your employees.

UNDERSTANDING THE ROLE PEOPLE-EMPATHY PLAYS IN ACHIEVEMENT

Achievement provides an employee with the opportunity to reach difficult, but attainable, goals. It is dehumanizing for an employee to sit all day at a repetitious task with no opportunity to change, or affect, the outcome of the job he is doing. If we define achievement in a "negative" manner, we can say that it is not "running faster and faster just to stay where you are." To give an example, we have an employee whose responsibility is to place a nut on a bolt as it passes him on an assembly line. If he usually accomplishes 50 attachments in an hour, we do not provide him with achievement by telling him he now has to make 100 in an hour.

If we manage with empathy, then we realize that achievement could be reached if the employee were given the opportunity to make the whole assembly instead of just attaching nuts to bolts. This way, the employee participates in a bigger portion of the job being done. Empathy tells us that as he performs at increasingly higher levels, he feels a sense of achievement in having reached a tough, but attainable goal.

Malcolm P. was the chief consultant for a major engineering firm, whose responsibility it was to coordinate with local governments in the site selection and construction of many projects. One area requiring much of his attention was bridge construction. Malcolm had three competent engineers working for him. Each was required to work on only a portion of a bridge project, while Malcolm did the final coordination. Looking at the situation with people-empathy, Malcolm P. realized that the engineers were becoming bored and restless. He decided to turn over complete responsibility for each bridge project to only one engineer and then rotate assignments among them. The result of his people-empathy was that his engineers consistently performed at increasingly higher levels. Malcolm's company began growing once again and his entire department enjoyed a handsome year-end bonus.

HOW TO PROVIDE RECOGNITION WITH PEOPLE-EMPATHY

The need for recognition is easy to satisfy, but one that is most often overlooked by managers. First of all, for recognition to provide motivation, it must be sincere and honest and must be done with empathy. Recognition takes many effective forms that say: "I saw you achieve, you did a good job, and I appreciate it." This is using empathy to make management pay off.

Obvious sources of recognition include the company publication, liberal use of the local press, and the thank you that a manager says when a job is well done.

Managers who use people-empathy have come upon one method of providing recognition that is not used nearly as much as it should. This is the note, or memorandum, sent to an employee recognizing a particular accomplishment and thanking him for his participation. If this note also includes copies sent to the next higher level of supervision and to the personnel folder, it becomes more meaningful. Recognition also can be achieved by having the employee sit down for a few minutes to become acquainted with his supervisor's supervisor. It also helps when managers from several levels up take the opportunity occasionally to visit the employees at their work stations for nothing more than a "hello" and a "how are you?" This is how empathy works; it allows a manager to recognize his employees. Most important is that empathy pays off when there is employee satisfaction. Motivated employees return dividends to the company.

Steve C. was appointed supervisor of an independent testing laboratory. Upon assuming his duties, he found his entire group seemed to have low morale and lacked motivation. A neighbor confided in Steve and pointed out that his predecessor liked to take all the credit for everything that was done. Steve thought the situation over using people-empathy. The next day, he began to sincerely praise his people. He wrote notes to them with copies to their personnel folders and to the director of the lab when something significant was accomplished. He made liberal use of the press to recognize his employees. Within weeks they responded; morale rose and motivation was noticed. The employees felt their lab was number one and they were right.

HOW RESPONSIBILITY CAN BE PROVIDED
BY USING PEOPLE-EMPATHY

The need for responsibility is an area in which modern management has come on strong. Contrary to early scientific management theories, employees do wish to seek increasingly higher levels of responsibility. This does not mean the same thing as being promoted to higher levels of management, but just becoming more responsible for the work which is being performed.

A manager provides responsibility for his employees if, in addition to the assembly function, he also establishes a system to allow the worker to perform the quality-inspection function. The employee now becomes more responsible since he also must determine whether his own work meets quality standards. To carry this one step further, the employee may also be allowed to sign his name to the unit he is producing and so state to the world that he has produced and inspected this unit and takes the responsibility for meeting quality standards. If we operate with empathy, we trust the employee enough to take this risk. We may get burned once or twice by some employees in the beginning but the resulting motivation will make it worthwhile.

Effective responsibility carries with it accountability. In managing with people-empathy, it is through this accountability that the employee feels responsible for the task that he is trying to accomplish. At first employees will be somewhat apprehensive when given responsibility; however, in time they will easily fit into their new role. The apprehension grows out of the fact that, for many years, they have had someone in a superior position making their decisions for them. Empathy helps us see this in our employees. Empathy helps us help the employee accept increasing responsibility as we remember that this is a new experience for him.

HOW GROWTH MAKES SUPERVISION PAINLESS

The need for growth exists in all of us, whether talking about advancement to a top level management position or expanding a job to include more than just soldering a connection. If we use empathy to its fullest, then we realize that true growth comes when an employee has an opportunity to do more. The employee becomes more involved and his work has more meaning for him.

Not every employee can, or even has the desire to, advance into increasingly higher levels in the organization. However, each employee does desire to have his work become more meaningful for him. There have been many themes on this aspect of employee needs. They have come out in such terms as job enrichment, job enlargement, and job rotation. Of these three, job enrichment truly provides the opportunity for growth. Job enlargement, stated simply, is "more of the same." A dishwasher who is assigned to washing knives has his job enlarged when he is given the responsibility of washing forks also. He is still a dishwasher and his responsibility is still washing silverware; he has not grown in his job. Job rotation provides an opportunity for an employee to see other types of jobs. But it does not provide growth in his present task and assignment. If we are to manage with empathy, we must recognize this important difference.

HOW SAM W. MOTIVATED HIS EMPLOYEES AND INCREASED PRODUCTION PAINLESSLY

Sam W. is the superintendent of the final assembly department of a company that manufactures a well-known automotive part. Three months after he took over the department, Sam knew that it had the highest rework rate of any department in the company. He spent the first few weeks getting organized in his job and trying to get a handle on the problem causing the large number of reworks. Eventually, Sam felt that he had diagnosed the basic cause of the problem. He was sure that it was due to a lack of motivation on the part of the workers, as well as their supervisors, to do better.

In a bold move, Sam called the employees together and discussed the productivity findings with them. Then he outlined his concept and thoroughly discussed it with them getting their inputs and opinions. As a result, he reorganized the department in such a manner that it allowed him to put in two more machines in each of the sections.

Each employee became responsible for completing the entire assembly process through the inspection phase in his section and for signing his name to the inspection tag stating it had passed quality control standards. The initial results showed a drop in productivity as the employees took on this new responsibility. However, as they became more comfortable in this new role, they increased their productivity by better than 30 to 35%. Rework was reduced from an all-time high of 31% to less than 4%. The initial cost savings from Sam W.'s department were most significant. As a result, the entire department consistently shares in a substantial bonus at year-end. What is more important, through people-empathy Sam has a department of highly motivated workers.

RECOGNIZING NEEDS WHICH DO NOT
MOTIVATE PEOPLE ON THE JOB

It has been found that money (salary), company policy, benefits, interpersonal relationships, and working conditions (work environment) are not sources of motivation. These items are so powerful in terms of creating dissatisfaction if they are not present to an adequate degree, they are often mistaken as being a source of motivation. However, before an employee can be motivated, these needs must be filled. If we manage with people-empathy, we realize that once these needs are filled, the employee has the capacity for concentrating on those things which *will* motivate him.

These critical needs have degrees to which they must be filled and can have varying levels of importance. For instance, if the work environment is not exactly pleasant, the employee can stand a lot provided all other needs are basically filled. The worker may be unhappy with the environment, but as long as it is posing no immediate threat to his safety and well being, he tolerates much more than if his other needs were not satisfied. However, when an employee's wages are not adequate, this poses a threat to his ability to provide for the safety and security of his family and becomes a more important need to be filled. It takes people-empathy to recognize this point: the more his salary is inadequate, the greater is his dissatisfaction. In some instances, the employee might seek work at another company where wages are more competitive; or the employees as a unit may seek the safety and security of a union to help them fill the void. But the important thing to note here is that by obtaining employment at another company, or voting a union into the current organization, the employee does not attain motivation. He is not "turned on" to the company because he has a union and he will have no incentive to work for the overall goals and objectives of the company. What the employee has done, in effect, is to find a third party who will help him reach the level of satisfaction needed.

HOW INCENTIVE PLANS DO NOT MOTIVATE

Many companies put all their eggs into one basket and try to capitalize upon the need of an employee to be paid an adequate wage through the creation of incentive plans. Incentive plans have seen a variety of forms. In many instances, companies have tried to establish individual, "piece rate" incentive plans to spur the individual employee to higher rewards as a result of increasing productivity. What most companies find when operating with people-empathy is that there is a level to which an employee is willing to work for the incentive. Beyond that, there is little or no activity. When incentives have been set on an individual basis, there is tremendous disharmony between the employee and the employer over the incentive standards. Usually, this disharmony results in a lack of achievement of the objectives of the company. There is not a cooperative effort to reach these goals.

This is not to say that all incentive plans are bad. Properly installed and developed incentive plans, particularly those that work on a group basis, have been successful in achieving productivity especially if they have been installed using people-empathy. However, in most instances, the incentive has resulted in a form of *recognition* rather than a means of making up an inadequate salary.

HOW DELMAR T. OVERCAME PRODLEMS
WITH INCENTIVES

Delmar T. was production superintendent for a large manufacturing facility. When he came to work for his company, they had piece-rate incentives that had been in effect for several years. One of the first things he noticed was that, as production superintendent, he constantly appeared to be acting as mediator for grievances and complaints regarding the incentive system. There were two major complaints concerning the incentive program: the company's standards were too tight; and the work that the previous department was sending along was too poor in quality. Each succeeding department claimed it was not able to achieve its incentive standards.

Delmar felt that there must be a better way. Therefore, he began a personal study of the situation using people-empathy.

In his review, he found that the standards were not too tight. However, as is usually the case, the company was reluctant to review the standards on a periodic basis to make sure that they were up to date. Delmar also found that it was a practice for a department, and particularly for each individual in the department, to turn out as many units as possible without consideration for quality. This helped to explain the high rejection rate in final inspection.

After studying the situation, Delmar called a meeting of his supervisors and discussed the situation with them and, as a result, developed several ideas. He began having a series of small-group meetings with his employees. Out of these meetings, he developed a concept of a group incentive that could be applied to all employees plant-wide. Basically, the incentives were established to pay off as a result of a plant-wide increase in productivity. It took approximately one year of careful study by the Industrial Engineering Department to set up the system.

In the first year after it was set up, the overall increase in productivity was 12%. The second year resulted in a 15% increase in productivity. Each year thereafter, Delmar realized an increase in productivity and the employees enjoyed a true incentive bonus.

HOW TO RECOGNIZE THE INFORMAL
ORGANIZATION

If all employees were fortunate enough to have all of their maintenance and motivational needs met, informal organizations would not exist. However, it would be a rare situation when an employee could have all of his needs met by the formal organization. If we are managing with empathy, then we know that the formal organization is limited. The formal organization can provide the employees with definite roles and specific duties. However, it usually satisfies only the more basic maintenance needs involving a source of income, safety and security, and a sense of belonging at its basic level. It can also provide a source of satisfaction for the motivational needs.

People-empathy helps us realize that although the formal organization provides a sense of belonging, most are fairly large (more than twenty to twenty-five people) in terms of an individual's intimate associates. The goals and purposes of a company appear to be something on the order of platitudes in the same category as "patriotism" and "mother love." Workers realize that they are helping the company to achieve its overall goals and purposes, but it is difficult for them to identify their goals with these goals. It is most difficult for an employee to identify his goals as being the same as those of his production superintendent—or even more remote, the president of the company. However, most employees can understand and identify with the problems, opportunities and goals of their peers. This is important for us to recognize and it takes people-empathy to be aware of this situation.

Managing with people-empathy, we can easily see that these peers are generally people of the same social background and circumstances. They are not only people who work together, but they are also the people who build friendships together. Managers might rub elbows with their employees at the annual company picnic, but due to the nature of the organization, those managers will remain apart from their employees. Therefore, an employee's socializing will be done among those with whom he feels most comfortable. The informal organization gives greatest satisfaction to the love and belonging needs that each individual possesses.

HOW PEOPLE-EMPATHY HELPS US
RECOGNIZE THE GOALS OF THE INFORMAL
ORGANIZATION

The existence of the informal organization does not, in itself, create difficulties. However, in managing with people-empathy, we realize that the conflicts which arise are over the goals and objectives as perceived by the formal and informal organization. When the goals and objectives of both groups are headed in the same direction, then no problem exists. People-empathy helps make us aware that when the informal organization sees its goals and objectives as being different from those of the formal organization, problems occur. In some instances, the differences in the goals and objectives will arise as a result of the informal organization misunderstanding what is desired of it in order to achieve the goals and objectives of the formal organization. However, in a few instances, the informal organization will feel that the formal organization is using and exploiting it and will deliberately direct its goals against those of the formal organization. Managing with people-empathy helps to avoid this situation.

One thing that is sure about an informal organization, it will develop its own leader. If the formal organization is departmentalized such that the informal organization actually is a series of sub-groups, each sub-group will develop its own leader. Usually management, when it operates without people-empathy, likes to think that the leaders of these groups are the supervisors that they have appointed over these areas. Actually, the informal organization usually rejects the leader selected by management. If the organization has a member of the informal organization in a crew-leader, or "working supervisor" position, he may or may not emerge as the natural leader of the group.

While the leader of the informal organization may not be the person with the most technical knowledge, he is the one with the natural leadership ability. This informal organization is operating with people-empathy. Because management often selects a person for leadership based on his technical skills, they miss the person with the natural leadership ability. This is the reason why the informal organization selects its own leader and why managers should develop people-empathy to gain maximum success in their operation.

There have been many supervisors who met failure by

trying to bull their way past the natural leader. In those instances where the natural leader has been recognized, supervisors have tried to put the heat on them to conform to their way of thinking, resulting in serious problems for the supervisors involved. This is where people-empathy could have helped the most.

HOW TO USE THE INFORMAL ORGANIZATION
FOR RESULTS—PAINLESSLY

For maximum effectiveness, it is necessary for the manager to use people-empathy and try to understand something about the informal organization. We have already talked about those things which go into the makeup of the informal organization. The first element in understanding an informal organization is the recognition that whether we like it or not, it does exist. And the second thing to understand is that it will have its own leader.

In order to manage with people-empathy, first determine whether a series of small, informal organizations resulting from a highly departmentalized company, or one large, informal organization exists. This must be determined because only then will you know whether you are dealing with one leader or several group leaders.

Next, find out what binds these groups together. Are all the members of the same department? Do the majority of the members of the informal organization have an interest in outdoor sports? Are the majority of the members male? Female? Are the members of the organization from a large metropolitan area, and thus from diverse backgrounds; or are they from a small town and do they have an immediate common interest? Once the common bond of membership is known, then you have made a step in the right direction with people-empathy. You know what is of interest to this organization; you know what will turn off this group to its management; and you are well aware of how to develop the interest of the informal organization in striving toward the goals of the formal organization.

The next step is to pick out the leader, or leaders. This may be a little more difficult because in the informal or organization the leaders, too, are informal. If the informal organization is loosely strung together, it will become more difficult to determine who the leader, or leaders, are. The more cohesive the informal organization is, the more readily identifiable will be the leaders. Once you have identified the leader, the most serious mistake is to play up to him and grant him special favors. This is not operating with people-empathy. The informal organization would immediately recognize his as being the "patsy" of management and would then seek out a new leader. To use the informal organization's goals and objectives to achieve the goals and objectives of the company, management must keep the leader informed and consult with him periodically as the representative of the organization. This tells the informal organization that you recognize him as their leader and nothing more. By communicating through him and with him, you invite the informal organization to work together with the formal organization.

HOW CHARLES D. LEARNED ABOUT
INFORMAL ORGANIZATION

Charles D. was the manager of a fabrication department in a company that made sub-assemblies for use by all the major manufacturers of general aviation aircraft. Charlie had three supervisors under him. One supervisor was responsible for the metal stamping department, another for instrumentation, and the third supervisor was responsible for the assembly line.

Charlie noticed that his supervisor of the metal stamping department was having considerable difficulty meeting his production quotas. The previous month, this supervisor made only 80% of his quota. When Charlie D. called the supervisor in, he explained the problems his lack of meeting quotas was creating in other areas of production. He also told him that it was going to be necessary for him to get his production up before the next month.

A few days later, Charlie decided to follow up with the supervisor, who explained that he had really given his department a sound tongue-lashing. Charlie thought about this but couldn't help feeling that something wasn't quite right. A couple of weeks later, it appeared that the supervisor was in even more serious trouble because production was going to be at an all-time low for his department.

Charlie talked to the supervisor and suggested that at the next coffee break the supervisor should have a cup of coffee with the actual leader of the informal organization. Charlie suggested that the supervisor might not want to verbally abuse this man, but instead communicate to him as the natural leader of the group. The supervisor was encouraged to take charts and graphs and actual data showing the problems that this particular department was creating on an overall basis.

The immediate results were not dramatic. However, Charlie guided the supervisor over a period of time in developing a communications link through the leader of the informal organization. By utilizing this leader, the supervisor was able to turn his production around and within three months to reach 100% of budget. During the last few months of the year, he really turned his group on so that they were able to meet their budget quotas for the year.

2

Maximizing Employee Achievement Through People-Empathy

One of the motivators of many employees is achievement. It appears that industry has tried to apply this fact equally to all workers. However, all men do not have the same urge to achieve. Many employees will be satisfied with their present situation within certain ground rules.

If you are to manage painlessly, it is extremely important that you use people-empathy when providing achievement for employees. It is through people-empathy that you recognize that employees are individuals and, as such, react differently to the urge to achieve. When managing with empathy, you realize that you cannot provide achievement to all workers with the same equality. In order to manage effectively with people-empathy, you must understand some of the characteristics of the urge to achieve.

PRINCIPLES OF PROVIDING ACHIEVEMENT

There are three basic principles to follow in providing achievement when managing with people-empathy.

1. Employees must be involved in setting their own goals and determining the difficulty of the task which they will undertake.
2. The goals chosen must cause employees to stretch in order to achieve the results.
3. Employees must feel they can influence the outcome of the task through their own efforts.

It is important that the employee receive adequate feedback so that he understands how well he is doing on his progress against his goals. The key to utilizing achievement as a means of motivating employees is people-empathy.

HOW EARNEST B. HELPED AN EMPLOYEE
ACHIEVE AND FOUND A SUCCESSOR

As sales manager for a medium-sized company, Earnest B. supervises the entire sales force through seven regional managers. Earnest knew that he was in line for promotion to vice-president of marketing. He also knew that before he could receive this promotion, he would have to select and train a successor for his position. Earnest B. had a successor ready, the selection process having begun two years earlier.

One of the regional sales managers had been turning in average performance for his territory over the previous five years. He consistently achieved 93% of his scheduled budget. His performance was not bad enough to consider termination, but it was not good enough to consider outstanding and did not rate him as one of the top regional sales managers. At the time, Earnest could not understand this since this regional sales manager was highly competitive in many activities.

Earnest B. analyzed the situation using people-empathy. He realized that he had been imposing the budget quotas upon the regional sales managers. Most of them had accepted these budgets and made every effort to achieve them. After reflecting with people-empathy, he realized that this particular regional sales manager could not accept these budgets. Therefore, prior to the budget sessions for the coming year, he held planning meetings with the regional sales managers. After discussing the situation, he found that the regional sales manager who was lagging was willing to set a budget that was at least ten percent higher than what would have been set for him. After the first six months this regional sales manager and his salesmen had topped the budget that was to be established for the entire year! This happened consistently and Earnest B. found that he had a top-notch successor in this regional sales manager. By having used people-empathy, he had assured himself of the promotion to vice-president of marketing.

HOW TO GIVE AN EMPLOYEE A COMPLETE, NATURAL UNIT OF WORK

When managing with people-empathy, we realize that some workers are not interested in achieving. It is necessary to identify those who have the strong urge to achieve. If the evidence from the work situation is not sufficient to point out the achievers, we can look elsewhere to find this information. The true achievers, who are not finding satisfaction in their jobs, will shift their primary interest to other activities such as the Boy Scouts, PTA, professional organizations or other activities in which they can satisfy their urge to achieve.

After identifying the achievers, go one step further with people-empathy in order to achieve painless supervision. You must provide these employees with a complete, natural unit of work. A person with a strong urge to achieve is not satisfied with an isolated job over which he cannot control the ultimate result of his tasks. An employee on the assembly line with one isolated task to accomplish, a switchboard operator with no relief from the routine of answering calls, or a junior manager who is not given the responsibility to make mistakes will find frustration with their tasks if they are achievement-oriented. It is important that people-empathy is used to make sure that the unit of work is *complete* and natural. Attempts to make a job interesting by adding more routine duties to the work of an employee will only extend his sense of frustration. Therefore, we must use people-empathy.

In order to manage with people-empathy, it is necessary to understand a complete, natural unit of work. As discussed in Chapter 1, a complete, natural unit of work is not achieved by adding *more of the same.* That is to say, if a worker is responsible for soldering one connection it does not make his job more complete to have him solder two connections. If we manage with people-empathy, we begin with the job description. Utilizing people-empathy, a manager constructs a job description for the individual employee so the task will involve responsibility and accountability for the job from beginning to end.

Many managers develop job descriptions based on the old Scientific Management System. Accordingly, jobs are reduced to the lowest common denominator. This means that each employee becomes a specialist in boredom—a specialist in overseeing checking accounts, a specialist in tightening bolts, a specialist in handling overdue accounts—all without responsibility. However, the manager who supervises with people-empathy and makes his job more painless ensures that his employees have broad responsibilities. Those working for such a manager have complete, natural units of work to accomplish and the responsibility and accountability that accompany such jobs. Those employees feel a sense of achievement each time they accomplish their job.

HOW LYNN D. DEVELOPED A PAINLESS TECHNIQUE FOR ENRICHING THE JOBS OF HER EMPLOYEES AND EARNED A BONUS

Lynn D. was the branch manager of a large bank, where

she processed many loans. This was because the bank's location served a large number of farmers, and it was located in the automobile sales district and was a convenient source of auto loans. Working for Lynn were two loan officers who had the responsibility for processing all loans coming into the branch bank. She set up a system so the loan officers would process the loans and bring them to her for approval. Because of this system, Lynn had the lowest bad debt ratio of any of the branches.

However, this system had its drawbacks. Although Lynn was top-notch in the area of the loans, she had no time to perfect her abilities in other areas of banking, nor did she have time to train the two loan officers to become her replacement. As a result, Lynn was not ready for promotion.

Sensing this and reacting with people-empathy, Lynn analyzed the situation. She decided to take a calculated risk: she turned over complete responsibility for the processing and approval of the loans to each of the loan officers. This would mean that the loan officers would have complete responsibility for the entire processing of the loans, including the responsibility for the bad debts that could be incurred as a result. She also began seeing that each of the loan officers would spend time with total responsibility for the branch during periods of her absence.

The results were immediate. Lynn not only had the time she needed to concentrate on those areas of banking where she was weak, but she was training a subordinate to replace her. To her surprise the bad debt ratio improved even further. Because of this and the efficiencies that resulted, Lynn earned a sizable bonus this year and was programmed for a promotion within the next six months.

HOW EMPATHY HELPS YOU GIVE AN EMPLOYEE MORE DIFFICULT TASKS

When we speak of achievement, we are talking about those

goals that cause an employee to "stretch" in order to reach them. If the goals are set too low, they will not create achievement; they will just be another task which the employee is performing within the scope of his routine chores.

To operate with people-empathy, we need to realize that not every task an employee does can be a source of achievement. Many of the day-to-day activities an employee performs will be routine and in some cases, boring. But these are necessary items and are not to be excluded from the activities. However, each employee should have goals that will be difficult to attain, and which are to be completed within the course of his job. But if we are to operate with people-empathy, we must know how to give these types of goals to our employees.

The principles of giving an employee more difficult tasks can be summarized as follows:

1. The employee must be a part of the process of establishing the goals.
2. The task, while difficult, must be reasonable.
3. The tasks must carry the necessary responsibility and authority.
4. The task must have a definite date for completion.

People-empathy helps us to realize that when we assign a task, no matter how difficult, to an employee without his participation, we minimize the chance that this task will be viewed as an opportunity for achievement. There may be a lack of commitment. The employee may view this project differently and may not hold the same sense of urgency as his supervisor does. Our job becomes much easier when we use people-empathy. With people-empathy, we realize that we must sit down with our employee and discuss the goal. During this discussion, the employee can participate in establishing not only the task itself, but the standards of performance that will tell when a satisfactory job has been done. With people-empathy, we obtain employee commitment to the task; and when the task is completed the employee will feel a sense of achievement.

When we are setting goals with an employee, people-empathy helps us to realize that a goal must not only be difficult, but it must be reasonable. Even with employee participation, it is possible for a goal to be set that is so difficult that it can never be reached. Employees setting goals for the first time tend to be over-enthusiastic. It is here that we as managers must exercise people-empathy. This will help make our jobs much easier in the long run. If an employee is constantly faced with objectives that he cannot complete, he will become frustrated. People-empathy helps make our jobs as managers painless and helps assure that we reach our objective of providing achievement.

PEOPLE-EMPATHY HELPS US PAINLESSLY ASSIGN RESPONSIBILITY AND ACCOUNTABILITY

When we assign a task to an employee, there is a strong temptation to retain absolute control. In this way we feel that we can assure that the outcome will not only be favorable to the employee, but to us as managers. However, if we are to operate with people-empathy, we must turn over the necessary responsibility and authority to the employee. It is by this means that an employee feels a sense of satisfaction and achievement. Initially, this will make for trying times. But managing with people-empathy will make supervision painless because it will build trust and confidence. It will also free us to take control of other more meaningful projects.

When we are establishing goals and objectives for our employees, people-empathy demands that we establish a time by which the task is to be complete. Without a time limit, the employee will establish his own schedule, even though it may be a subconscious effort. All objectives and goals will be loose and at the whim of the employee to perform. This means that some projects may be finished within one day and others within one or two years. By the time the projects are complete, the results may no longer be needed; however, managing with people-empathy establishes a timetable with the employee so that he knows when the task is to be complete. This provides another measure for the employee to determine if he has truly achieved his goal. Therefore, we take one more step to ensure that we are operating with people-empathy. This will make our supervision painless.

MURRAY T. PROVIDES HIS EMPLOYEES AN OPPORTUNITY FOR ACHIEVEMENT

Murray T. was the advertising director for a large department store. He was responsible for the total advertising program for the main store and each of its three branches. Working for him were three artists and a copywriter. He also had an advertising manager at each of the branches.

To assure that the advertising reflected the image that the department store wished to project, Murray required all prospective ads for each of the branches to be submitted through him. This meant delays during those periods when Murray was on vacation or sick. It also meant that an additional measure of planning was required on the part of the branch advertising managers when they were mounting a campaign.

The advertising managers at the branch stores got together and asked for a meeting with Murray to discuss the problem. After hearing the complaints of these managers, Murray began to think about the situation. The more he thought, the more he realized that his managers were right. Then Murray began looking at the situation with people-empathy.

Murray T. set up a program so that his managers would be responsible for all advertising at their individual branches. They would have complete responsibility and accountability for submitting proposed advertising campaigns through the artists and copywriters and back to themselves for appropriate usage.

The only time that Murray would become involved was when a scheduling problem arose and he would have to set the priorities. He would manage his managers and rate them on their overall performance throughout the year. This program was effective and the results were dramatic. Murray T.'s advertising department consistently won every major advertising award in his area. He also placed high in national competition for the types of advertising campaigns from his department store.

PROVIDING SPECIALIZED TASKS ALLOWS EMPLOYEES TO BECOME EXPERTS

When we manage with empathy, we recognize that it is important for an employee to become the "company expert" in a particular area. In becoming the expert in his field, an employee has the opportunity to increase his exposure to more levels of management and broader cross-functional lines. A manager must operate with a special kind of empathy in order to make specialty assignments effective. This does not mean that tasks are to be reduced to the lowest common denominator. Rather, people-empathy helps us provide specialized assignments with complete responsibility and accountability.

In order to establish the proper concept of management with empathy and make our jobs as managers that much easier, let's consider four principles for developing specialization in task:

1. Look at the entire function of the department and not just the job description of the employee.
2. Look at the employee's past and current performance appraisals for strengths and weaknesses.
3. Through discussions with the employee, determine his areas of interest.
4. Make the task meaningful but sufficiently difficult so that the employee will have to strive for achievement.

In looking for an opportunity to help an employee achieve, look to the function of the entire department rather than just to job description to make assignments with empathy. The individual job descriptions may be rather narrow in scope and we risk missing potential opportunities if we limit ourselves to this area alone. If we look to the broad scope of the entire department, we may find exciting areas that will be extremely interesting to the employee and beneficial to the department.

As managers supervising with empathy, we must look at performance appraisals for areas of strength and weakness. If we do not look at the performance appraisals, we may assign an employee a task before he is ready to handle the situation. It is true that we may want to use the opportunities afforded us to broaden the skills of the employee and strengthen areas of weakness, but we do not want to put him in over his head. We want to look at areas where we can capitalize upon the employee's immediate strength as we broaden his base of knowledge.

In offering an opportunity for an employee to specialize, look at areas that will be of interest to the employee. We do this with empathy, and this makes supervision that much easier. If we look at the areas of interest for the employee, we provide him an opportunity for achievement and success. An employee will find more motivation from achievement in an area of interest than he will from an area which he finds extremely distasteful.

In managing with people-empathy, we must assure ourselves that the task that we are assigning the employee is meaningful to him. Although the area may be of interest, we can find ourselves overloading the employee in unnecessary detail that offers no advantage to the employee himself. As in all areas of achievement, the task should cause the employee to reach for his goal. When the employee strives to accomplish the task, he will be provided with achievement. Empathy tells us that we must not place the task out of reach of the employee. Rather than providing motivation, specialization will provide only a sense of frustration for the employee if he cannot reach his goals.

People-empathy is important in providing specialized tasks for an employee. If we use people-empathy, it will make our supervision painless; we will see our employees and our departments grow. We, ourselves, will grow and achieve.

TERRY D. EMPATHIZES WITH HIS
EMPLOYEES TO PROVIDE ACHIEVEMENT

Terry D. was the manager of the pensions and annuity department of a medium-sized insurance company responsible for providing actuarial data to the field, receiving and disbursing funds from various accounts, and working closely with investment personnel responsible for the funds for various pension and annuity accounts.

Under him, Terry had three pensions and annuity supervisors. Each supervisor handled assignments based on a workload/assignment basis.

Terry noticed that in many instances his supervisors had to consult with one another. As he followed this through, he found that each supervisor felt more comfortable in one particular area. Therefore, when a supervisor was handling a problem in which he felt uncomfortable, he logically would consult with his counterpart, who was the expert in that area, for information. Terry D. also noticed that many other department heads were not always satisfied with the answers his supervisors were giving them unless the answer was in that particular supervisor's area of expertise. Terry sat down and went through the four principles of assigning specialized work.

After this, he began making assignments based on the area of expertise and interest of each of the supervisors. As department heads would come with questions or a need for information, he would ask the supervisor with the expertise in that area to handle the problem. His supervisors began receiving a lot of praise and were accorded the titles of experts. His department increased in efficiency. At year end, because the changes were so dramatic in his department as a result of using people-empathy, Terry D. received a higher than normal merit increase.

HOW TO PUT ACHIEVEMENT
TO WORK FOR YOU

The key to putting achievement to work is people-empathy. It is people-empathy that helps us recognize the urge to achieve in our employees. It is through people-empathy that we perceive the challenges that will cause our employees to strive for higher goals. Let us look at the elements involved in putting achievement to work:

1. Recognize the urge to achieve in the employee.
2. Determine what challenges cause each individual employee to respond.
3. Develop those activities which are of interest to the employee.
4. Capitalize upon the expertise of the employee.
5. Work with the employee and be wary of dictating goals for achievement.

If we are using people-empathy, it is essential to determine if an employee has an urge to achieve. Many times, an employee may have reached a level at which he feels confident and beyond which he feels there is nothing further for him. If we try to key upon an achievement urge that is nonexistent, then we are liable to frustrate our employees. If we recognize the achievement urge in those that have it, and capitalize on it, then we will have employees who will strive to higher levels of performance in our department.

In recognizing the challenges that sustain performance in an employee who is achieving, we must recognize what the individual goal holds in store for the employee. In other words, people-empathy says that we must recognize what "turns an employee on." We must recognize what will tell the employee when he has achieved, and we must understand what will bring the employee to higher levels of performance. It is when we analyze the behavior of each employee and determine how he paces himself toward achievement that we will be able to operate with people-empathy and make our supervision painless.

When putting achievement to work for us, we must ensure that we are looking into those areas of interest to the employee. The employee must be interested in what he is doing if he is to receive the satisfaction of achievement. This means that we must look at all available areas and activities under our control through which we can utilize possible achievement for the employee. The areas selected for achievement must capitalize on the area of the employee's expertise. The employee without such an area of expertise can develop one by being allowed to operate in his area of interest. The important thing is that an employee must be allowed to work in an area that will strengthen his capabilities. He will feel a sense of satisfaction as he is relied on as an expert.

Finally, we must ensure that the employee participates in the decisions that lead to these activities to provide achievement. As long as the employee participates in these decisions, he will feel that the goals are realistic and meaningful. He will feel that he has been treated with people-empathy and will feel that the way chosen is the way he would do it. This is one method of making sure that we have employee cooperation in our activities.

HOW JAMES C. LET HIS EMPLOYEES BUILD A WALL AND FOUND THAT THEY COULD ACHIEVE

James C. was a general foreman of a construction company. He had a theory that if the walls were set correctly, the rest of the building would be easy. Because of this, he was always on the job measuring, using a level and observing wall construction through his theodolite. He was constantly giving instructions to the workers and to his foreman to ensure that the walls were perfect. This, of course, created problems whenever James was sick or out on vacation and meant that a section of construction had to wait until his return. Because of this, deadlines were sometimes missed and penalties would often have to be paid. His walls could not be faulted, however, and his construction methods were perfect.

Jame C.'s boss, the owner of the construction company, was a person skilled in people-empathy. He had a long talk with James and explained what he observed and told him that he respected him for his ability as a construction engineer. His boss pointed out that it was essential that they reduce the number of deadlines missed in order to get their costs down due to penalties being paid. They talked about the situation and decided upon a course of action.

On the next construction project, James turned over complete responsibility for the construction of walls to the workers. During this construction phase, he made it a point to be absent from the project so that he would not be tempted to offer advice. He went to another construction site to look in on other phases of activity that truly required his presence. When the wall was done and James had inspected it, he found it had been done better than he could have done. In talking to one of the foremen, he found out that the employees readily accepted the challenge because they maintained all along that they could do the job better than James. Without realizing it, James C. had stumbled onto a source of achievement for his employees. However, the credit would have to go to the owner of the company who actually guided James C. through the principles of providing for achievement. It was a lesson well learned, and as a result, all future projects saw substantial reduction in overrun times. As further incentive, the company owner provided James with a bonus out of the profits resulting from the reduced costs from the reduction in penalties.

3

How to Utilize
People-Empathy to
Increase Employee Growth

All employees do not necessarily desire to advance to higher levels in the organization. However, each employee desires more meaningful work. People-empathy makes supervision painless when we recognize this need in an employee. The manager who uses people-empathy redesigns those jobs reporting to him, within the framework of existing technology, to make them more meaningful. The goal is to make the job interesting and thereby to give the employee more initiative and control.

Those managers who supervise with people empathy have found that growth has proven to be the most effective management tool for increasing performance and satisfaction. Employees who have jobs that contain more than routine tasks and who have the discretion to exercise responsibility and authority are generally found to be more productive. This is especially true when compared to those employees whose jobs have little opportunity for growth.

When supervising with people-empathy we must use five basic principles of providing employee growth:

1. Assign an employee something new.
2. Recognize the difference between providing growth and job enrichment.
3. Give up some of your authority.
4. Provide for advancement.
5. Let employees work on special projects.

HOW TO ASSIGN AN EMPLOYEE SOMETHING NEW—PAINLESSLY

An employee can find satisfaction in his job providing he feels that what he is doing is basically important. This requires the manager who operates with people-empathy to keep his employees informed as to how their jobs contribute to the success of the company. This may mean that the supervisor will have to provide reports and information to his employees; it also means giving employees decision-making responsibility.

In every company, jobs tend to become so familiar to an employee that detailed instructions are no longer necessary. If this situation is allowed to progress further, an employee can become discontented. A manager operating with people-empathy will know that growth can be the solution to this problem.

In seeking to overcome the problem by providing growth, a manager must use people-empathy to ensure that he does not overwhelm the worker. To provide an employee with something new, painlessly, there are five steps that should be followed:

1. Have the employee participate in the decision to take on something new.

2. Let the employee know the importance of the new task to the company.
3. Be specific in what the new assignment is to cover.
4. Set difficult but attainable goals.
5. Give the employee decision-making responsibility.

HOW MARY W. LET HER EMPLOYEES HAVE MORE RESPONSIBILITY AND FOUND TIME TO DO THE THINGS THAT REALLY NEEDED HER ATTENTION

Mary W. was the local manager for a national firm of certified public accountants. Working in her office, she had three auditors and two management consultants. Initially, she had set up the organizational structure and responsibilities so that when an auditor went out on a job, he would turn over his results to her and she would assign whatever assistance needed from the management consultants. This also worked in like manner when management consultants went on an assignment. Although the results always met the quality standards expected by the parent firm, her operation tended to have many inefficiencies.

After this problem was brought to her attention on her performance appraisal, Mary began looking at the situation with people-empathy. She viewed the situation by what was expected of her and what she was demanding of her employees. After having reviewed the organization with people-empathy, she realized that she had a golden opportunity. Mary began assigning her employees complete responsibility for all those things affecting their job. If a particular assignment required consultation with another auditor or management consultant, it would be up to the individual concerned to make proper coordination.

Over the period of the next six months she saw an immediate increase in the efficiency of her operating group.

After operating with people-empathy for a year, she was given a much deserved promotion to regional vice-president and her salary was increased to $30,000 a year.

HOW PARTICIPATION IN THE DECISION
WILL MAKE SUPERVISION PAINLESS

By participating in the decision, the employee will feel that the new task belongs to him. His participation will help ensure that he fully understands what will be expected of him. Participation will help the employee feel that he is making a contribution. This use of people-empathy will help you to treat the employee as the individual he is. This will show that you truly value his opinion, particularly when it affects his work.

By including the employee in the decision-making process, we provide an opportunity to include his thoughts in the process. By using only our thoughts, we may be restricting ourselves and not looking at the problem creatively. Many times an employee, who is closer to the situation than we are, has good ideas to offer. Therefore, when we structure something new for the employee, people-empathy helps us include his ideas so that what we are providing will be growth for the employee. These concepts are important if our supervision is to be painless.

WHY THE EMPLOYEE SHOULD KNOW THE
IMPORTANCE OF THE NEW TASK

Until the employee can recognize the importance of the new assignment to the company and to him, it will not encourage employee growth. If the employee somehow feels that the task he is doing is meaningless, he will feel frustrated. On the other hand, if he knows he is making a contribution, he will feel a sense of accomplishment when he has completed his task. Therefore, we must use people-empathy so that we will be specific with the employee concerning the importance of the new task to the company. If we cannot take this step in our own minds, then people-empathy demands that we abandon this particular assignment as a means of growth and look to others.

In order for us to let the employee know how important the job is to the company and to him, we must keep him informed. The best sources of information are reports issued by the company and various departments within the company. Many times we overlook a source of information for our employees. If we manage with people-empathy, we will make these reports available to the employee. This becomes critically important when the employee accepts the new task so that he can realize the impact of his assignment on the company.

BEING SPECIFIC ABOUT THE NEW
ASSIGNMENT HELPS MAKE OUR
SUPERVISION EASIER

Speaking in generalities when defining the new task to the employee may often leave him confused. It is easy for us to talk in concepts and generalities because it is from these broad-brush thoughts that we, as managers, develop the overall goals and objectives. But until we are ready to get specific, we should not try to hold a meeting with the employee. A manager operating with people-empathy will outline specific goals and recommendations before his first meeting. These goals and recommendations may be modified during the discussion, but by being specific, we offer a framework for the discussion. We must allow for corrections and recommendations to come forth. If we talk in generalities, we may not offer the employee enough information to be able to participate fully. It takes people-empathy for us to provide an opportunity for a meaningful discussion on the new assignment.

The specifics of the job assignment will be the framework upon which the employee will know when the standards of performance have been reached. This is necessary to keep the employee from being frustrated. If we talk in general terms, we may have one set of standards while the employee may visualize that he is expected to perform at another level. When the task is complete and the employee feels that he has met the standards of performance, but we know that he has not, he will become frustrated. This may puzzle the employee and he may refuse to accept new assignments in the future. We will not have provided employee growth; instead we will have turned him off.

WHY WE MUST SET DIFFICULT BUT ATTAINABLE GOALS IF WE SUPERVISE WITH PEOPLE-EMPATHY

Anytime we are involved in setting goals, we should recognize that the objective should be an improvement over what is being done now. When we set a goal that is too easy to meet, we remove the sense of excitement and achievement. If we manage with people-empathy, we recognize that if there is an element of difficulty involved, the employee will be proud of the accomplishment. This is true of the new assignment itself, but there is a problem here: because the assignment is new to the employee, it may be easy for us to set the goals too high. If our employee becomes frustrated over his inability to reach his new goals, he may lose the desire to work well at anything.

When we sit down with our employee to have a discussion, we must be sensitive to the enthusiasm he is displaying. Utilizing our experience and working as managers who use people-empathy, we must guide the employee to realistic goals, goals to challenge his creativity and cause him to reach out and become a star for the team. It is the difficulty in achieving the goal that will cause the employee to feel that he has grown. It is through the use of people-empathy that we increase production rates and quality levels.

HOW TO GIVE THE EMPLOYEE DECISION-
MAKING RESPONSIBILITY

In assigning an employee something new, we may feel that it is easy for us to retain the responsibility for making the decisions. However, if we do this, we may rob an employee of an important opportunity to do something on his own. If we manage with people-empathy, then we realize that he should have the responsibility for the decision, no matter which way it goes. Then the employee has an opportunity to learn and to build self-confidence. Any person, whether he is a child growing and learning, a worker on the shop floor, a manager of a branch bank, or anyone who has someone exercising supervisory authority over him, will grow more and more dependent upon that person if he is not allowed to make decisions on his own. This takes away the self-confidence of the individual. Then given the opportunity to make a decision, he may run in fright.

When we manage with people-empathy, we give the employee the opportunity to make decisions in the new job we have assigned him. We give him the chance for definite growth. He will grow in his ability to learn, and as he learns his decisions will become sound; responsibility will increase his self-confidence. As managers who use people-empathy, we recognize the importance that the employee attaches to responsibility. The employee will accept this responsibility and will research his facts as he begins to gain confidence in the new assignment.

HOW JANE P. GAVE HER EMPLOYEES MORE
NEW AND DIFFICULT TASKS AND INCREASED
DEPARTMENTAL EFFICIENCY

When Jane P. took over as Marketing Vice-President of her company, she found that she had some immediate problems. Her predecessor held the job for an extensive period of time before he retired. Because of this, he was something of a "father figure" to his employees, but his methods were terribly outmoded and often promoted inefficiency.

After she had been there only a few weeks, one of her employees came to her. Product manager for one of the largest sections of her company, this employee had been with the corporation for four years, was making a very good salary, had a nice expense account, and exercised considerable authority over the product line. However, he was growing bored and dissatisfied. The former Vice-President of Marketing had assumed that with all the Product Manager had going for him, he would be content to stay in his position throughout his career.

Jane P. managed with people-empathy. She understood what the problem was and how this employee was stifled through lack of growth. Jane realized that she would have to go slow in making some changes, but changes were in order. She began assigning her department managers new and more difficult tasks. Sometimes these tasks took the form of special projects; at other times they involved taking up the slack in areas belonging to other departmental managers. She did this after carefully consulting with the managers and gaining their input.

Under her guidance the managers began to grow. The product manager became ready to take over as her new sales manager. Other managers began to grow and move into positions of higher responsibility. Her department moved from operating inefficiently to a department with the highest efficiency in her company. Jane P. easily marked herself as a rising executive soon expected to take over the company presidency.

RECOGNIZING THE DIFFERENCE
BETWEEN PROVIDING GROWTH AND
JOB ENRICHMENT

It is true that job enrichment can lead to growth. But if we manage with people-empathy, we know that job enrichment should not be mistaken for growth itself. In providing for growth, we as managers who use people-empathy may seek to use job enrichment as one step along the way; but we also recognize that growth comes from more than job enrichment and the two are not really one and the same.

Job enrichment usually results from a one-time activity. The employee's job will be increased such that he will be given more meaningful responsibility for the time the activity is being performed. Growth, on the other hand, is an ongoing affair. The employee must be given goals with increasing responsibility. Initially, job enrichment accomplishes this; however, when we manage with people-empathy, we recognize that we must go beyond job enrichment. The involvement will cause the employee to stretch himself and "grow." This includes everything from job enrichment to promotion.

When job enrichment came upon the scene, many managers jumped on the bandwagon feeling that this was the answer to all their employee problems. They wanted to use it as a cure-all. However, those managers who use people-empathy recognize it for what it is—a tool to be used along with others. As with any tool, job enrichment has its limitations.

Myron V. was enchanted by job enrichment. He joined the bandwagon and enriched the jobs of all his employees. The initial results were astounding, but it wasn't long before Myron was pressed to come up with bigger and better things. At this point, he began to manage with people-empathy. He looked beyond job enrichment to include those things that provided growth for his employees. With his new outlook using people-empathy, Myron V. became a more effective manager and was rewarded by a salary increase of five thousand dollars at the end of the year.

CARL J. PROVIDES GROWTH FOR HIS STAFF
WORKERS THROUGH EMPATHY

Carl J. was general manager of the Fire, Auto, and Theft Division of a large insurance company. Due to the company organization and because it was by nature a marketing-oriented company, Carl had mostly staff men reporting to him. He had been unusually successful in picking competent people to work for him, and any one of his employees was capable of stepping into his position.

As usually happens, the role of being in an advisory position can sometimes lead to frustrations. Therefore, it takes a manager with people-empathy to provide staff-type employees with growth. Carl J. was a manager who used people-empathy.

Carl began with job enrichment. Then he included those jobs that gave increasing responsibility. Carl J. acquired the reputation of having the best division staff in the company. His managers grew, and so did he.

HOW GIVING UP SOME OF YOUR AUTHORITY CAN MAKE YOUR JOB EASIER

Many managers find it easy to retain all authority for activities in their area. Because they will ultimately be held responsible, they feel that this retention of authority will give them complete control. In some instances, managers feel that only they have the knowledge for some of these activities and it is necessary for them to retain authority. This usually comes from the feeling that it is more difficult and time consuming to pass the needed information along than to do it yourself. However, this is not operating with people-empathy.

If we operate with people-empathy, we realize that our employees need the opportunity to have authority of their own. It is this authority, attained through people-empathy, that will help provide achievement for them. It is also providing them with authority that will make our jobs as managers much easier. It will free us to do the things that really need our attention as efficient managers.

When we manage with people-empathy, we realize that when we give our employees responsibility they must have the authority. They must have this authority before we give them complete accountability for the job they are doing. If we refuse to give them this authority, we in effect "ham-string" them. Then they can only go so far without our assistance to help them complete the task. With people-empathy, we give our employees the authority to do the job. Then, they are able to do a complete job and this provides growth. When the job is done, the employee feels a true sense of accomplishment. This can only be done if we properly use people-empathy.

HOW LARRY E. WORKED HIMSELF OUT OF A JOB—AND BECAME DEPARTMENT MANAGER

Larry E. was a section manager for a large chemical company involved in the manufacture of pesticides. Larry was a manager who instinctively used people-empathy with his employees. When Larry set up his department, he looked at the goals and objectives necessary in order to do a successful job. Then he sat down with those who reported to him and discussed how, as a department, they were going to contribute to the success of those goals and objectives. When the discussion was finished, each of his subordinates had readily accepted his portion of the task. In addition to giving them the responsibility for these opportunities, he gave them the authority to carry them through to completion. In some instances, the authority was budgetary; in other instances, it was to make the final decision on projects. He made sure that these subordinates understood that they had the authority to coordinate activities that were necessary, even if it involved other departments or sections.

As a result of his utilization of people-empathy, Larry was able to visit other department managers and section heads and discuss their problems with them. He also discussed the way they viewed their needs from Larry's department. This established him as being a person sensitive to the needs of the organization as a whole. As a result, he could operate without having "blinders," or "tunnel vision" and could give appropriate guidance and counsel to his subordinates.

The management of Larry's company appreciated this. It was only a short period of time before they recognized his true talent and promoted him to the position of department manager. With this promotion his career was well launched in his company.

HOW LETTING EMPLOYEES WORK ON SPECIAL PROJECTS PROVIDES FOR GROWTH PAINLESSLY

One of the ways in which a manager can use people-empathy to help provide his employees with growth is to assign them special projects. Special projects are those beyond the scope of the normal goals and objectives, or daily routine, of the department. These projects will usually involve special research on the part of the participant. In many instances it will require special coordination with other departments or groups. These projects can provide the employee with an opportunity to learn something new and to demonstrate his ability to others in the organization.

We need to look at the principles of assigning special projects through the use of people-empathy. These principles are as follows:

1. Ensure that the project is meaningful.
2. Have the employee participate in the initial discussion.
3. Handle the project with target dates and standards of performance.
4. Give the employee the necessary authority.

When we begin to develop a project and we feel that we would like to assign it to an employee, we should establish that it is, in fact, meaningful. This will involve thinking through the project and determining its overall effect on the organization. It just may be possible through the use of this thought process that we find the project is not as significant as we thought; we may avoid wasting valuable time. At any rate, we will help prevent assigning an employee to an overstated project. It doesn't take the employee long working on a project to realize that the results will be of little use to the organization. The result will be that the employee will not feel a sense of accomplishment or growth. However, if we use people-empathy, then we will be sure that the results have significant impact on the organization; and the employee, as a part of this project, will experience growth.

After we have a basic outline of what the project is to accomplish, we should involve the employee in the preliminary discussions. These preliminary discussions will allow the employee to provide his input and thinking, and will also allow him to hear the thinking of those who conceived the project. In this way, the employee will have a full understanding of what he is to do. If we do all the leg work and preliminary activity ourselves, we will have reduced the project to no more than routine paperwork that any technician could do. The employee will feel a strong sense of growth if we have used people-empathy and have allowed him to participate in all stages of the project, including the preliminary stages.

When we assign the project to the employee we should handle it just as we would any objective and goal. That is, if we are using people-empathy we will assign target dates and establish standards of performance with the employee. Again, it is essential that the employee be a part of this decision. He can well establish the timetable which he will be able to follow; this way he will be living with something he believes in. Additionally, by establishing the standards of performance, he will have had the opportunity to fully realize what will be expected of him. When we have done this with people-empathy, the employee will feel the sense of growth that goes with the special project when it is completed.

If we are going to have the special project provide growth

for the employee, it is necessary that we give him the complete authority necessary to get the job done to meet the standards of performance. Again, if we do not provide this authority, we reduce him to no more than a clerk assembling data on a page for us to complete. With authority, the employee will feel a true sense of growth and achievement when he has completed the assigned task.

HOW PAUL W. DEVELOPED A DEPARTMENT MANAGER PAINLESSLY BY ASSIGNING A SPECIAL PROJECT

Paul W. was production manager for a large manufacturing company. One of Paul's department managers had been promoted and assigned to a division in another city. Paul needed to fill this gap in order to continue to provide the effective management his company needed. He had one candidate whom he felt was a strong contender for the position, but Paul was unsure of his ability to sell his selection to top management.

Paul decided to work with people-empathy. He knew that his company was having problems in the production process that needed to be resolved. So he decided to appoint his candidate to the position of temporary project team leader. In this position, the candidate, along with a team of three other people, would have the authority and the responsibility to carry out the necessary actions to resolve the problem. By properly assigning this special project with people-empathy, Paul assured the candidate of every opportunity to prove himself as the person to fill the open position.

At the end of three months, the project team leader reported the results of his findings with recommendations. These recommendations caught the eye of top management. When Paul then made his recommendation to them for the new department manager, they readily accepted it. People-empathy helped Paul select his department manager and made his supervision painless.

PUTTING GROWTH TO WORK FOR YOU THROUGH EMPATHY

When we put growth to work for ourselves, we must use people-empathy. It is through people-empathy that we realize those activities that generate growth. We understand that the same activities will not provide the same growth to each of our employees. It is with people-empathy that we know how to assign an employee something new. When we use people-empathy, we realize that job enrichment does not necessarily provide growth although we do understand that job enrichment can be one step toward growth. We then can successfully combine our efforts with job enrichment to provide sincere, honest growth for our employees.

When we operate with people-empathy, we provide growth through additional responsibility. We give our employees the responsibility for the tasks they are doing as well as the authority to accomplish these tasks. It is when we fully provide this responsibility and authority that we operate with people-empathy. In managing with people-empathy, we realize that we must give up some of our authority to provide growth for our employees.

People-empathy helps us to overcome the urge to control the infinite details of all projects and activities we assign an employee. We know through people-empathy that for the good of the employee, the department and ourselves, we must relinquish authority to the employee. We recognize that this is not the same as abdicating our authority for the operation of the department itself.

When we manage with people-empathy, we provide advancement for our employees if they are to grow. We often feel that because an employee is doing a good job where he is, we cannot afford to lose him. However, with people-empathy we realize that we cannot afford to keep him in a position forever. We assign our employees special projects so they can grow. The use of special projects can help an employee learn new and different tasks and enable him to become an expert. These methods require the careful use of people-empathy for the employee to feel the sense of growth that comes from the accomplishment of the tasks to which he has been committed.

4

Guaranteeing Yourself Constant, Reliable Feedback

HOW LISTENING EFFECTIVELY CAN
MAKE SUPERVISION EASIER

In order to listen with people-empathy we must cooperate in our effort to communicate. Listening with people-empathy helps develop the understanding that the words being used might have different meanings for people based on their particular experiences and environment. We must give consideration to the subtle variations in meaning, the structure used to convey the meaning, the emotions of the speaker, and the attitudes conveyed by the tone of the speaker.

To discover the importance of people-empathy in listening, we need only think about a typical day. As much as 80% of our day is spent listening to someone or having someone listen to us. Now let us think of some of the things that might have gone wrong during a typical day. Many times these difficulties result from communications not being heard, or else the communications were received in a distorted way because we did not listen with people-empathy.

Listening with people-empathy is perhaps the most dif-

71

ficult task we have facing us as managers. Since the objective in listening is to comprehend what the speaker is saying, we are faced with the possible conflict between our preconceived judgments and decisions and those of the speaker. We are distracted by background noises or activity, actions by the speaker, temperature, pictures on the wall, and our own physical feelings. To compound the problem, we think faster than we can talk. Most of us talk about 125 words per minute, we can listen about three times as fast, and we can think approximately four times as fast. This gives us plenty of time to think. These thoughts are usually brief side trips to a more pressing problem or pleasant memory. Then our thoughts return to the speaker.

When we listen with people-empathy, we do so with an open and receptive state of mind. Listening with people-empathy is an art. In order for us to listen with people-empathy, we must make a voluntary effort to comprehend what we hear. Only when we are receptive to what is being said can we give our full attention. Successful listening can lead to understanding, and understanding will help make our jobs as supervisors easier.

In order to listen with people-empathy, we must be aware of ourselves. We must give of ourselves to the communications; we must expend a great deal of energy to listen productively and remain involved. We must be able to examine statements critically, evaluate them, and make comparisons against the attitudes and relationships of the speaker.

Not only must we listen with people-empathy, but we must know how to listen intelligently. We must successfully listen while digesting what is being said. Effective listening involves four basic skills:

1. Organizing the spoken statement as the speaker proceeds
2. Determining the main point and supporting point and reasons

3. Summarizing effectively
4. Avoiding the distractions of background noise, accent, emotion, length of the discussion, illustrative materials, pictures on the wall.

In order for us to communicate with people-empathy, the speaker, the listener and the statements being made must be mutually related. The person transmitting and the person receiving the information must know what they are trying to understand. The content of the communications as well as basic facts must be agreed upon. Both the speaker and the listener have a mutual responsibility to communicate with people-empathy and to ensure there are no breakdowns.

Since we depend heavily on being able to communicate, listening without people-empathy can lead to frustration. When we say something, we want it to be understood and accepted. When we receive an indication that our listener understands and accepts our statements, we are gratified and receive a certain amount of pleasure. An improper response from the listener can be taken as disapproval or rejection. If this occurs over and over when we are listening, the employee, or group of employees, will be likely to feel frustrated. Successful communications take place when both the person transmitting and the person receiving the information use people-empathy to reach the same level of agreement with respect to the information given.

Here is a typical example of a communications problem arising from difficulties in listening. It illustrates the point that when people from different environments orient their listening to their own way of thinking, the results are less than satisfying.

A small research organization was acquired by a larger company. It had been fairly successful in its operation because the scientists and technicians were free to innovate. The stockholders of the small company wanted to realize capital gains and long-term appreciation, and the acquiring corporation wanted to diversify.

After the merger was complete, the large corporation

found that the financial situation of the research organization was not as good as it thought. Immediately, the president imposed controls using textbook methods. When he spoke to the new organization to explain what he was doing and why, he *assumed* that they were as grounded in the fundamentals of business management as he. The research organization did not understand what he was saying. They assumed that he was attempting to stifle their creativity, and he promptly began to lose key scientific people.

Fortunately, the president was a person who operated with people-empathy. Realizing that both sides did not have a common frame of reference for communicating, he called in a third party who could help both sides listen with people-empathy. Knowing what they faced, and being responsible people, the scientists dug in and brought the company back to a profitable position.

We are using people-empathy if we see and listen to others as they appear realistically. We must see others as distinct personalities with their own beliefs, thoughts and wishes. This means that we must make every effort to affirm the integrity of those with whom we are listening.

When listening to others, we must strive toward mutual understanding. Our listening must become highly selective as we become more aware and attuned to the essence of the facts or situation at hand. There must be a full acceptance of the other person as he is. If we listen to what our employees are telling us and understand how the communication seems to them with its personal meaning, then we will be moving to establish effective communications through people-empathy.

We must create a situation in which we come to understand each other from the other person's point of view. Such understanding comes through people-empathy and can be initiated by either party without the other person participating. Listening with understanding and people-empathy can help eliminate defensive exaggerations and "false fronts." Understanding through people-empathy leads to the discovery of truth; it leads to a realistic appraisal of the subject being communicated. Mutual communications through people-empathy move toward solving the problem rather than creating others. If we use people-empathy, we must see how the problem appears to the other person as well as to ourselves.

HOW GEORGE H. LEARNED HOW TO LISTEN AND GAINED THE ENVY OF HIS FELLOW SUPERVISORS

George H. was the personnel manager for a small corporation. He had personnel responsibility for a plant involving 300 people. During the period when wage/price guidelines were in effect, he needed some information relative to salary administration, and he had to see a member of the accounting department in order to get the information. The accountant was an expert on the guidelines and George knew that he would give a lengthy explanation of a complex and intricate rule. At the outset, George began to apply the four basic skills of listening effectively. He made sure that he brought a pencil and paper to the meeting.

During the conversation, George made every effort to organize the spoken statement as the accountant proceeded. He did this through the effective use of questions about the matter under discussion.

As the accountant was talking, George jotted down the main points and the supporting points and reasons. Where there were still areas of confusion, he asked questions in order to further clarify the issues. When the conversation had finished, George summarized what the speaker had said. He did this so that the accountant would have an opportunity to correct any misunderstandings. During the entire conversation he made every effort to concentrate on the accountant himself and on the written notes he was taking in order to avoid all distractions in the office.

As a result, George was able to put together the most effective salary administration package in the history of the company. He became the envy of his fellow personnel managers at other plants and locations. He was well thought of by the employees at his plant and gained the respect of management as being a manager operating with people-empathy. The ultimate result was that George was promoted to the position of Corporate Industrial Relations Manager with a salary increase from $18,000 to $25,000 a year.

HOW DEVELOPING EMPATHY
HELPS CREDIBILITY

The best results in obtaining feedback through people-empathy grow out of personal integrity as seen and accepted by our contemporaries. The effectiveness of feedback is commonly assumed to depend upon the people-empathy of those who deliver it. Whatever the contents of feedback, it will be accepted and acted upon only if those doing the communicating have done so with people-empathy. Exercising integrity and establishing rapport are highly complex human achievements and can only be attained through people-empathy.

A young man ordered an item from a local hardware store. As luck would have it, the item was temporarily out of stock. After waiting patiently for a week, he called the store to see if his order had arrived, and the salesman reported that the delivery of the item would be made within 48 hours. Some four days later he tried to explain to the outraged customer that his supplier meant 48 working hours, not clock hours. The result of not communicating with people-empathy was a double loss of integrity—that of the supplier, and that of the hardware store. It is vitally important when people are managing others and conducting a business to develop credibility through empathy.

Approval of a statement by highly respected persons or organizations gives it the same integrity as if the person said it himself. If we as managers allow statements to be made in our name, we will allow our employees to create the same credibility in their minds toward the statements as if we had made them ourselves. The integrity of a statement depends upon the people-empathy person making the statement.

There is more required of the transmission of information than the common framework of language. We must assure that the transmission of information is done with people-empathy; the meaning and intent of what is being communicated must be accepted. The most critical factor for the acceptance of the meaning and intent is the integrity and the relationship that exists between those who are exchanging the messages. This integrity can only be achieved through people-empathy.

Our ability to accept the statement made by another person depends upon how well informed and how intelligent we believe that person to be with regard to the statement being made. This requires a high degree of people-empathy. There is a qualification to this: if we feel that the person communicating with us is informed and intelligent enough to make valid statements on the subject discussed but we suspect him of being motivated to making an untrue statement, then we will reject his communications. The weight that we give to a statement based on these qualifications determines the credibility of that person and comes from the empathy achieved with the person.

Leadership through people-empathy can be taken as an indicator of expertise and knowledge. The statement "right from the top" confirms our belief in this fact. A foreman can go into the mill, or a branch manager of a bank can go to his teller and make a statement to those supervised, and it may or may not be accepted. If these same people make the same statement but quote the general manager or bank president, the possibility of acceptance is increased. If the general manager or the bank president makes the statement himself, acceptance probably will be immediate.

If we as managers constantly use people-empathy in all our activities, we will increase the likelihood of generating trust between ourselves and those we supervise. Trust between individuals, however, does not automatically exist.

When Sam took over the accounting department, things went well initially. Then he began putting in extra hours after work. Before long, he was working through the weekend. His supervisor felt that he might need more help and put through a special requisition for another accountant. This didn't help since Sam continued to drive himself harder. Before the supervisor could get to the bottom of the difficulty, Sam had a nervous breakdown. He required lengthy treatment before he was well enough to return to work.

During Sam's absence, the manager investigated the situation to find out what had driven him to a nervous breakdown. Upon talking to the accountants in the department, the manager found that they had little to do to keep them busy and what work they did was no more than routine bookkeeping. Most of the work in the department was done by Sam. It appeared that he did not manage with people-empathy and could not let himself *trust* the others in his department to do the work. Sam's lack of people-empathy and distrust caused a loss of effectiveness among his subordinates because he could not communicate with them when it mattered.

JIM W. GETS INFORMATION THROUGH EMPATHY AND IS CONSIDERED THE COMPANY RESOURCE MAN

Jim W. was a plant manager for a large food products company, but he could not have taken over this position at a more inopportune time. The previous plant manager had left to join another firm and Jim had to take over in the middle of a union campaign.

Jim W. was a manager who used people-empathy in all his operations. Because of this, he was able to communicate well with his people and develop rapport. The workers respected him and trusted him, and as a result, they felt they could communicate with him. The feedback he was getting helped him put together complete, reliable information. As a result, he turned around the union election.

Because of the reliable information he was getting and could provide the top management of the company, he was considered a resource man. Jim W. managed with people-empathy and had developed such a tremendous degree of trust with the employees that he was promoted to the position of division general manager.

HOW YOU CAN USE QUESTIONS TO GET
RELIABLE FEEDBACK—PAINLESSLY

The usual way to get information is to ask a question. Questions are windows to the mind. In an appropriate situation we have probably felt like asking, "What do you want from this communication? What do you expect? What would you like to accomplish?" If we were to ask these questions straightforwardly with people-empathy, in addition to other information, we would probably succeed in finding out the other person's needs and what he is after. Then we could guide our communications accordingly.

When we ask a person *why* he reached his conclusion or *why* he did what he did, that person's defense mechanism will take over. He will rationalize and present a good argument supporting his reasons why. Rationalizing is a defense mechanism which we all resort to in some form or another when presented with the question "why."

When we develop a recommendation which we really want to see implemented, we review the possible questions that might be asked; and one of the first questions we anticipate is "why." Usually we are right. Someone asks why we want our recommendation put into effect and we provide the justification. If we are to operate with people-empathy, the next time someone presents a recommendation, we should ask him "how," not "why," he arrived at his conclusion. We will overcome his tendency to rationalize and will bridge the gap in communications. Furthermore, we will offer that person a chance to review the logic that went into developing that particular recommendation.

The proper use of questions in communicating as a means of recognizing needs generally involves these decisions:

1. What questions to ask
2. How to phrase them
3. When to ask them

The importance of properly phrasing a question is well illustrated by the following story. A clergyman asked his superior, "May I smoke while praying?" Permission to smoke was emphatically denied. Another clergyman, approaching the same superior, asked him, "May I pray while smoking?" To the question thus phrased, permission to smoke was granted.

The use of questions is a powerful communications tool and must be employed with people-empathy. The question determines the direction in which the conversation, argument or discussion will move. The proper use of the question through people-empathy can often take command of communications. The question we ask also controls the amount of information likely to be given back to us, much as turning the water faucet controls the flow of water. Questions stimulate other persons to think, and they often start thinking critically about the topic of the communications.

By asking a specific question, such as "What time is it?" or "Do you like watermelon?" we are demanding only a limited amount of specific information. Such questions are usually easy to answer, and in essence we are guiding or controlling the thinking of the party. However, if we go to the other extreme and ask a general question such as "Why did you do it?" or

"How did you do it?" then the answer is more difficult. Answering such questions forces the person with whom we are communicating to think a great deal more—with the increasing possibility that he will re-examine his premises or more critically re-evaluate yours.

By asking questions with people-empathy we can easily secure immediate attention, maintain interest in the item under discussion, and direct a course that we want the conversation to take. Often, through the use of questions with people-empathy, the other person can be led toward the conclusion we desire.

It is a good practice to use people-empathy and to explain the reason for asking the question whenever this is feasible. It avoids trouble and embarrassment. Another way of preventing unnecessary or unpleasant emotional response is to avoid asking forcing questions like "What is your excuse?" By using people-empathy we might ask a nonforcing question, such as "How do you feel about this matter?" This kind of question permits full and continuing discussion.

Communicating with people-empathy is like erecting a building. Preparatory information corresponds to the supplies for the building. If we send the supplies to the site without plans having been previously furnished, the workmen might easily go ahead and put up any type of structure, not knowing what the architect had in mind. The correct procedure is for the architect to send the plans of the building to the job site first, and then when the supplies arrive, the workmen will (we hope) put everything in its correct place according to the plans. In using questions with people-empathy, we must give the other party a plan, in advance, of what we intend to gain from the conversation. If they have the plan first, then we can feed them the information, asking questions as we see fit. Ask questions with people-empathy and they will respond with much, if not all of the information in a proper perspective.

When we ask questions with people-empathy, we avoid those questions that carry any vague implications, or that can easily be turned to our disadvantage. Tone of voice and wording are given careful consideration. This is important in the interest of clarity and in order to avoid any false inferences. Questions asked with people-empathy are not asked to score an advantage, but for clarification. Well-conceived questions—concise and direct to the point under discussion—are powerful communication tools for discovering the motives and recognizing the needs of others, and they enable us to manage painlessly through people-empathy.

HOW JAMES R. LEARNED TO ASK THE RIGHT QUESTIONS AND BECAME A TOP MANAGER

James R. was a city manager for a nationwide chain of grocery stores. There were ten stores in his city and he was responsible for the operation involving a large quantity of inventory and sales.

Not long after James took over as city manager, it appeared that his job was in jeopardy. He never had the complete information necessary for the successful operation and management of those stores reporting to him. He always had a problem in getting accurate information. When information did come to him it lacked timeliness. His regional vice-president placed him on notice. However, the regional vice-president was a manager who used people-empathy. He was able to counsel James in the proper use of questions. The vice-president helped him develop a technique for getting the most out of his questions so that his information would be accurate and reliable.

During the six months that he was on probation, James effectively employed the techniques he learned with people-empathy. It did not take him long to become one of the most knowledgeable managers in the company.

A year after James R. was released from probation, he had moved from a person whose job was in jeopardy to a regional vice-president's position. As a result of using people-empathy, James became a top manager in the company and ensured his position as a growing manager.

HOW TO KEEP YOUR ASSUMPTIONS FROM BLOCKING INFORMATION OUT

It would be impossible for us to live from day to day without forming assumptions. We would not have enough time to move through our routine chores if we had to test each assumption that we had ever formed. When we see a chair, we assume it will support us. When we see an open door, we assume that we will pass through it when we cross the threshold. When we see the cooking eye on an electric stove glowing red, we assume that it is hot.

If we manage with people-empathy, then we will realize that we form assumptions about a person when we communicate with him. We know through people-empathy that we can assume either he knows something about the subject being communicated, or he doesn't know anything about the subject at all. If we assume that he knows something about the subject, then we must make an assumption about the degree of knowledge. We might assume that this person is biased about the subject, or that he is neutral about it. We might assume either that he is receptive to our communication, or that we are not getting through to him. With people-empathy we can continue to make assumptions until we have formed a body of *assumed* knowledge about this person and about our communications with him.

We have all been victims of our assumptions. But this does not mean that we cannot rely on our assumptions. What it does mean is that when our assumptions are based on incomplete information, there is a likelihood that we could be led astray. If our information is erroneous, our assumptions are likely to be wrong. If we base our information on facts that have been previously tested by us or others throughout time, then we are operating with people-empathy and our assumptions are likely to be right.

When we are using people-empathy, we will be sure that our communications will not go astray because one or more of our assumptions made during the communications process are wrong or inaccurate. We will use people-empathy to distinguish between fact and fiction, between fact and inconclusive observation, or between fact and inference. We realize that because a statement was made does not mean that such a statement is fact.

There is nothing wrong with making assumptions based on incomplete data, inconclusive observation or inference. If we use people-empathy, we must include these facts. When we use people-empathy we state our conclusions in such a manner that those to whom we are communicating will know that we are not certain. That way they will be free to make their own judgments about the conditions we have stated.

We may not be able to test each assumption in our daily lives, but when we are obtaining information, we can test some assumptions to ensure that we communicate effectively. As a matter of fact, in using people-empathy we must make these tests. There is a simple way of using people-empathy to test facts that will help us stay on solid ground. This is the effective use of questions.

Questions used to test the basis on which we have formed our assumptions will stimulate the communications process if we use people-empathy. These questions will help us establish rapport and we will become interested in the subject being communicated.

Teachers who have developed people-empathy have learned that questions can promote understanding of a topic being communicated. They are taught to ask for questions; they sometimes offer to let the class interrupt the discussion whenever there are questions. These teachers using people-empathy know that when they are asked questions, the likelihood that those listening will form erroneous assumptions is lessened. The way in which questions are asked can cause problems when testing our assumptions if we are not careful enough to use people-empathy. A salesman knows that he uses people-empathy when he asks, "Would you like to be one of the many lucky people owning our new product?" and he is more likely to make a sale than if he asks, "You wouldn't care to buy our product, would you?" By asking questions about the customer's product similar to the one being offered, about the absence of such a product around the home, about the customer's taste in this product and other questions of this type, the salesman can test his assumptions about the customer's need and desire for his product.

In order for questions to be asked with people-empathy and to help us test our assumptions, they should be gentle. They should go only deep enough to gather facts necessary to draw valid conclusions. Questions should be controllable so that answers won't stray; they should be direct and to the point. We should prepare the other person by letting him know why we are asking the questions. Questions are for clarification, not to produce a winner in a word contest. The only advantage to be sought through questions is effectiveness in communication and the achievement of people-empathy to help make our supervision painless.

HOW TED F. OVERCAME HIS TENDENCY TO ASSUME AND BEGAN GETTING COMPLETE, RELIABLE FEEDBACK

Ted F. had recently been promoted to the position of regional sales manager for an office products firm. In the field as a salesman, Ted had been an outstanding performer. He consistently managed to turn in record sales and was considered by all in his company as a person marked to move up to the top.

In his new position as sales manager, however, he somehow missed translating some of his best marketing techniques into effective management techniques. He accepted most of the information given to him at face value. This put him into a sticky situation, more often than not, because of his assumptions. He constantly found himself having to explain his way out of a situation developed from misinformation.

Because Ted was a top-notch person, and because he operated with people-empathy, it did not take him long to decide to test some of his assumptions. He did this in the same way that he did as a salesman. He used effective questions to clarify points and to test the assumptions to make sure his information was correct. It was through his efforts in using people-empathy that he was able to get complete, reliable information. He re-established himself into the winning pattern he achieved as a salesman. His supervision was painless and he earned a promotion to national vice-president of sales.

HOW COMPLETE, RELIABLE FEEDBACK
CAN HELP YOU OBTAIN RESULTS EASIER

People have an intense desire for information. Information provides the means for us to satisfy our need for knowledge. We can make sense of the world around us when we understand how things stand.

If a supervisor is operating with people-empathy and has established a good working relationship with his employees, he will know what the grapevine is saying. If the relationship is one of mutual trust, the employees will confront the supervisor with what the grapevine is saying. When they do this they are looking for verification of facts, not a shrug of the shoulders from the supervisor. It is important that the supervisor use people-empathy and provide timely feedback to the employees.

The realities of life do not bless us with the ideal situation or clear-cut cases that follow the textbook pattern. Suppose we are faced with the situation where the information is confidential. We must communicate on the one hand and remain silent on the other. There are things we must do if we are to use people-empathy—and we must do them or we run the risk of letting the grapevine take over.

A supervisor using people-empathy will contact his boss and let him know what the employees are saying. This will give top management an opportunity to sort out details that can be given to the employees. The supervisor must be prepared to answer a certain amount of questions the employees are bound to ask, and an action plan must be drawn up for providing answers.

The supervisor operating with people-empathy can then call in his key employees and give them the information. He can talk it over with them and get their reactions. By doing this, he will be using people-empathy and he can ensure that the right word is passed along. He is also provided with feedback that will tell him what additional information he may need to seek.

If the supervisor is using people-empathy, then he will give his employee the information straight and accurately. He will not try to "soften" the information if it is bad, and he will not play it up too much if it is good. To do so would distort the information and build up false hopes. Honesty is still the best policy in passing along or receiving information.

A supervisor using people-empathy never passes the buck. As an individual, he may have his own personal feelings about a matter and he should express these feelings to the right people at the right time. However, when communicating to the employees, he is still looked upon as a member of management. If he openly discusses his opposition to the stand management takes, he may be the hero of the moment, but he will eventually be looked upon as an "outsider" of the management team by his employees. His effectiveness will be diminished as a supervisor because this difference of opinion will provide a source of error.

Using people-empathy with both the formal and informal means of communication is important, and we must be prepared to take maximum advantage of both. If we don't, our feedback will be found lacking. If we do, then we will be operating with people-empathy and we will find that our supervision will become painless.

5

Building Employee
Responsibility and
Accountability Painlessly

People-empathy is the key to building responsibility and accountability in our employees. Successful managers realize the importance of providing accountability and responsibility and they recognize the importance of using people-empathy in achieving these goals. There are four principles to use:

1. Remove controls from your employees.
2. Increase the accountability in your employees.
3. Give your employees additional authority.
4. Make reports and records directly available to your employees.

REMOVING CONTROLS MAKES SUPERVISION EASIER

When we accept the responsibility of managing an operation, it gives us cause for a certain amount of concern. Those to whom we report are going to hold us accountable for the operation of our department. Therefore, it appears reasonable for us to retain as much control over all jobs reporting to us as possible so that we can ultimately influence the outcome. In managing with people-empathy, we realize how we feel if our supervisors do not give us the control for operations that are under us. As managers who use people-empathy, we must give consideration to those who report to us and be sure we give them control over their operations.

In order for an employee to feel that he is getting what he seeks out of his job, he must have the opportunity to take full control over that job. When we move an employee into a position, we must make sure that it includes this challenge. As managers operating with people-empathy, we know that there can be nothing more frustrating than to have a supervisor who will not give us control over the job which we are to perform. If we as managers do not give our employees the opportunity to control their job, we will kill all motivation to do a good job because it isn't really his—the job still belongs to us.

HOW PAUL C. BENEFITED BY REMOVING CONTROLS

Paul C. decided to open a large real estate/insurance agency. He had 45 employees working for him and he supervised with people-empathy. The usual custom in Paul's city was for the agency owner to retain final authority for approval of all sales. In using people-empathy, Paul gave all of his agents, whether real estate or insurance, control over their sales. He felt that as trained agents they knew as much as he did about the conduct of a sale. Because he did use people-empathy, Paul's agency became the number one operation in the city within a year.

In operating with people-empathy, we as managers can start by analyzing the jobs which we have under us. We must look in detail for the controls which we may have put on the job. At times these controls may be hidden, but we must seek them out to make sure that we have not inadvertently placed some controls on an employee. We want to be especially sure that the employee will not be constantly checked on the job that he is doing. When we manage with people-empathy, we ensure that the job will be done by the employee and not by someone checking on him.

As managers using people-empathy, we see that to motivate a man we must give him the responsibility that should be his. We do this by giving up the constant control that can rob him of the needed effectiveness. When we give him this responsibility with people-empathy, we make our jobs as managers easier. We will also gain a bonus—we will have time to do the more meaningful things that our job demands of us. These are the important things which we feel that we do not have time to do when we are controlling the jobs of those under us.

The essence of people-empathy that helps us give the needed control to our employee is pride. This is the pride an employee feels in accomplishing a task over which he had total control and responsibility. From our own experience, we know the pride that is felt in accomplishing a task over which we have total control. With people-empathy we remember these experiences and give the same consideration to our employees.

Hank was a manager who did not always supervise with people-empathy. When he took over his department, he wanted to make sure that he fully met the objectives that were given to him. Therefore he set up a series of controls so that he could have ultimate influence on the outcome of the activities of his department.

After two years in his job, Hank realized that he wasn't going anywhere. He met the objectives as they were given to him but he was not able to contribute that "something extra" to the company that was needed to brand him as an outstanding manager. Then Hank began looking at the operation with people-empathy. He decided to give some of the responsibilities directly to the employees reporting to him. This way, he would have time to do those things that would qualify as "something extra." Within one year's time, Hank had earned himself a $3,000 raise and a promotion to the division staff.

The key to providing control to our employees is people-empathy. It is the use of people-empathy in providing control that makes our jobs as managers easier. It gives us the opportunity to grow as managers; as our employees achieve, so do we. We can do those things, then, that gain the attention of management and help us move up in the organization.

HOW LEONARD H. REMOVED CONTROLS ON HIS EMPLOYEES AND FOUND THEY COULD DO MORE THAN EXPECTED

Leonard H. was the branch manager for a consulting engineering firm. When he first took over the position, he was almost overwhelmed by the tremendous amount of details. To make sure that everything was taken care of and all details were given proper attention, he established controls for every phase of the operation. Because of the number of engineers reporting to him and the variety of jobs being done at any given time, Leonard had his work cut out for him. He was constantly having to work 18 hours a day and most of the weekend just to stay abreast of the situation. He had not missed a contract date, but he had a few close calls.

Leonard was talking to one of the corporate managers. During the discussion he explained his situation and the amount of time he had to spend on the job. The corporate manager was a person who used people-empathy; he listened attentively to Leonard and quickly spotted the problem. He immediately recommended that Leonard try to remove some of the controls and turn over responsibility to the employees themselves. This frightened Leonard at first, but he decided to give it a try before he had a nervous breakdown.

Within six months after removing the controls from the

employees, Leonard had a highly efficient organization. Once in a while, he even found time for a golf game with some of the clients. Because he was efficient and could give the time to the clients that was needed by his position, he was able to increase the business in his office quite substantially. At year's end, he reaped the rewards of his effort in a healthy bonus that was 25% of his annual salary.

HOW TO INCREASE ACCOUNTABILITY IN EMPLOYEES—PAINLESSLY

So far, we have been talking about responsibility and giving it to our employees. Now we are going to talk about accountability. For some people the distinction is small, but it is an important one. A job description contains the responsibility that an employee has. Moreover, supervisors and managers may assign additional tasks which increase the scope of responsibility.

It must be remembered that by increasing the accountability in our employees, we are not passing on any of our accountability. We are still held accountable for those responsibilities given to us by our supervisors. But by assigning accountability to our employees for those things for which they are responsible, we offer the opportunity for them to build growth into their jobs.

If employees are not used to being accountable, we are sure to scare them to death if we do it all at once. Therefore, it is important that we plan our strategy through people-empathy for giving employees accountability. As a matter of fact, there are several steps which we can follow in assigning accountability:

1. We must carefully review the employee's job description for those items for which he is already accountable.
2. We should review the departmental goals and objectives for those activities in which the employee can participate.

3. On the initial go-around we should decide on one, or at the most two, items for which we are going to assign accountability.
4. We must sit down with the employee and carefully explain to him what it is that we expect of him. We must include standards of performance which will be used to judge his success. We must be careful to explain to the employee that this is not just another task to do or not to do. We must explain to the employee that we are holding him accountable for the success or failure of the assignment.
5. We must make sure that the employee clearly understands that we are not "tossing him to the wolves." We must make our resources available, especially in the initial stages, to help him over some of the rough spots. We will guide him, but we will not perform the task ourselves. With people-empathy, we do not lay it out so plainly that the employee has his task reduced to routine.

HOW GIVING EMPLOYEES ADDITIONAL AUTHORITY MAKES THEM EASIER TO SUPERVISE

In managing with people-empathy, we realize the importance of giving employees the authority necessary to accomplish the job. If we assign our employees accountability, then it is essential that we use people-empathy and give our employees the authority to accomplish a task. If we as managers retain all authority in our area, then we will stifle the growth of our employees. If we retain all authority, then we assure ourselves of constant disturbances to make decisions in areas that have been assigned to our employees. On the other hand, if we use people-empathy we assure ourselves the opportunity to have time to do those things that really need our attention.

One thing that must be pointed out here if we are to manage with people-empathy is the difference in giving our employees authority and "abdicating" our own authority. This may seem elementary, but it is a line which must be drawn. However, some managers, especially new ones, find it most difficult to draw this line. This may come from a lack of true understanding of people-empathy.

In operating with people-empathy, we know that we should give our employees authority to do a job. By the same token, we know that we do not give up our authority as managers. This now goes back to the area of accountability. What we are trying to do is to give our employees more responsibility. To do this, we give them the authority to get the job done, but we also hold them accountable for the success or failure of the project. However, it is important to remember that we are accountable to our supervisors. Therefore, we cannot just dump the entire responsibility for our area in the laps of our employees and then sit back and see what happens.

When we give our employees the authority to do the job, we must make it clear to them that we retain the final authority to review the success or failure of the project. When we manage with people-empathy, we must also make it clear that at any point where we see that more than the outcome of the project can suffer from action being taken by our employee, then we have the right to intervene. Such action should be reserved as a drastic measure where we see that serious disruption to the operation of the department or company may result.

When we give our employees authority to get a job done, we must carefully define the scope of that authority and its limits. Most employees will assume that any authority given to them is not unlimited. When we operate with people-empathy, we recognize the need in our employees to know where the limits are. If we take the necessary care at this step, we can avoid needless embarrassment for our employees and for ourselves at a later time. This embarrassment, and possibly frustration, can arise from the employee not having used enough authority, as well as from having used too much. Since this is the first opportunity our employees have had to exercise their authority, they may be a little timid. They will need the encouragement and guidance that we can give them from experience plus our knowledge of where the boundaries lie.

HOW TOM G. INCREASED EFFICIENCY BY 30%

Tom G. was the plant manager of the sausage division of a large meat packing firm. When Tom took over this position, he noticed that the foreman always came to him for all the decisions that had to be made. These decisions might include whether or not to work employees overtime, which lines to shut down for maintenance, whether or not to purchase ice from an outside vendor or shut a line down until the ice-making machine could be repaired. For all practical purposes, the foremen were messengers between him and the workers.

Tom was a manager who used people-empathy. He reviewed the situation to see what could be done and then began having individual meetings with each of his foremen. Gradually, he gave them the authority to make the decisions that affected their operations. For instance, the foremen could make the decisions on whether or not to work overtime. They knew what their production goals were, and they realized the economic limits within which they had to operate in order to achieve these goals. This included a careful monitoring of the overtime situation. Tom worked this way in all the other areas.

The results were outstanding. Within a short span of time he had increased the efficiency of his operation by at least 30%. This won him the attention of top management and it was not long before Tom was promoted to manager of production for the entire meat packing operation.

HOW MAKING REPORTS AND RECORDS
DIRECTLY AVAILABLE HELPS EMPLOYEES
TO BE MORE RESPONSIBLE

As managers, we receive many reports and records to tell us much about the company and the state of the business. These reports and records help broaden our ability to do our job. The principal means through which this is accomplished is knowledge. By knowing the status of various operations of the business we are able to plan and coordinate our activities more effectively to the benefit of the company and its objectives. We do not doubt the need for, and the importance of, these reports and records in order for us to accomplish our tasks. This is true unless, of course, there are too many reports and records and we do not have time to digest their contents.

However, as managers we often miss an opportunity to exercise people-empathy. If these reports and records are important to us in the conduct of our job, why would they not be important to our employees? If we are to operate with people-empathy, then we must make these reports and records available to our employees as far as possible. When our employees are well informed about the operations of the company, especially those that directly involve them, they will be better able to participate in helping achieve its goals and objectives.

At the outset, it is important for us to note that we do not necessarily have to make *every* report and record that is generated available to each employee. The important concept is that we are keeping our employees abreast of the situations that affect them. The further down in the organization that we encounter an employee, the more narrow in scope this information will have to be.

As managers who operate with people-empathy, we will carefully sift through the information that we receive and pass on what is meaningful to our employees. This does not imply that we will exercise censorship by passing along only good news, or information that *we* want our employees to hear. On the other hand, it is not necessary to pass on to each and every worker a copy of the corporate budget for the year. Although this might be information the worker finds nice to know, he is more concerned with the budget for his department and how it affects him.

One source of information which many companies are finding beneficial in passing along to employees is feedback from the customer. Many times, the employees of a company are isolated from the customer; and therefore, it is difficult for him to visualize the impact of his efforts. Customer feedback, both good and bad, lets the employee know the results of his work.

Companies often go to great expense to provide quarterly statements to shareholders on the operations of the company. Without going to quite the same expense, we can use people-empathy and provide the same type of information to our employees. Supervisors can hold regular meetings with their employees to pass on information concerning the state of the business. Stockholders' reports are provided to let the individual shareholder know the soundness of his investment. However, our employees have an investment in the business too; they are pursuing their careers here and have just as much need and desire to know the state of the business. By providing this information, we can also point out to employees what they can do to improve the business. If we generate a monthly report of activities in our department, there is no reason why we should not make this information available to our employees. After all, they participated in the accomplishment of these activities. Therefore, if we are managers who use people-empathy, we will make this information known to our employees.

If the quarterback of a football team is told that his objective is to score more points than the opponent, but all information as to how well he is doing is withheld from him—he does not know whether or not he is making first downs, touchdowns or being thrown for a loss—he will soon become frustrated and is liable to quit the game. In like manner, if we tell our employees they have certain goals and objectives to meet, but withhold information that indicates the effectiveness of their actions and progress toward these goals, we can frustrate these employees. The essence of operating with people-empathy is openness. As managers using people-empathy for painless supervision, we must provide all available reports and records to them for information purposes. In order to make this information meaningful, we may have to condense it or rephrase it in terms which apply to these employees. At all costs, we must avoid a show of giving employees information which in reality is meaningless. It will not take our employees long to realize that we are being something less than candid with them. This is where people-empathy helps make our supervision easier. We know what information to provide and when to provide it in order to help make our employees more responsible. When our employees grow in responsibility, then our jobs as managers become much easier

HOW ERIC F. HAD HIS EYES OPENED
TO PEOPLE-EMPATHY

Eric F. was the managing editor for a metropolitan newspaper. He had a fairly large staff of employees working for him. Throughout his career, he had always been impressed with the need for not passing along any information to his competitors. He had always worked under the philosophy that very little information was passed along to him; he was told just enough to get his job done and nothing more. Now that he was managing editor, Eric was using the same philosophy with his employees.

On a particular Saturday, a few assignments were muffed and deadlines were totally missed for the Sunday edition. In analyzing the reasons why, Eric realized that he was basically to blame. He had not given his employees enough information to do a thorough and adequate job. He had not made vital reports and records available to his employees from which they could determine the impact of their operations.

After this event, Eric had his eyes opened to people-empathy. He began operating with people-empathy and making reports and records directly available to his employees. Because of his move to people-empathy, Eric was able to produce more meaningful news. It wasn't long before the publisher recognized the abilities in Eric and promoted him to the position of assistant to the publisher with greatly expanded duties and responsibilities, as well as a substantial increase in salary.

HOW RESPONSIBILITY CAN HELP MAKE YOUR JOB EASIER

When we manage with people-empathy, we are aware of the fact that providing our employees with responsibility helps make our job easier. When our employees assume responsibility, they begin to operate more independently of our decisions thus freeing us to do the jobs which really should require our attention. When we provide our employees with responsibility, we allow ourselves the opportunity to review the strengths and weaknesses of our employees. It will become that much easier for us to capitalize upon our employee's strengths and to help strengthen the weaknesses that exist. Additionally, we will be able to pick out those employees most likely to succeed us.

In operating with people-empathy, we know that providing our employees with responsibility gives them the opportunity to truly participate in the objectives and goals of the department. In this manner, our employees develop a sense of accomplishment and growth. They develop a realization that what they are doing is truly meaningful. Without people-empathy, it is difficult to provide them with this responsibility. When our employees are provided with responsibility, they become motivated to do a better job and to accept even more responsibility. This use of people-empathy not only benefits us as managers, but the department and the company as well.

6

Empathy Techniques for Providing Recognition and Improving Performance

Sincere recognition tells us how others feel about us as persons. All of us like to be recognized as being a part of the organization because this gives us a feeling of belonging. We also like to be recognized for achievements that contribute to the success of the organization. When this recognition is provided, it makes us strive for more achievements. Our employees also like to be recognized as being a part of the Company and to be told when they have done a good job. In order to be effective, recognition has to be given with people-empathy and it must be sincere and honest.

Equally important, when recognition is given in the form of praise, it has to be deserved. An employee knows when he has merited praise, and he cannot be fooled by our attempts to congratulate him over trivia or when it is not truly deserved. With people-empathy, we can provide our employees with the recognition they need and desire. People-empathy makes it that much easier for us in providing sincere recognition for our employees. Recognition is an important tool in motivating employees; and if we are to use recognition as an effective means of providing motivation, we must use it with people-empathy.

HOW TALKING WITH EMPLOYEES PROVIDES RECOGNITION WITH EMPATHY

One of the best sources of recognition we can provide to our employees is talking with them. It shows that we think of them as being more than an employee number or clock card. This type of talking, however, must be done with people-empathy because it involves more than just issuing the orders for the day. Talking that provides recognition involves holding conversations with our employees. We must discuss things that interest the employee, we should be interested in his personal goals and ambitions, and we must be interested in his family. The most effective form of this type of conversation is a one-on-one situation which involves only the employee and us. Also, to be effective, these talks must be conducted more than once a year at performance appraisal time. Being interested in our employees is a year-around affair. We must use people-empathy if we are to be effective conversationalists with our employees such that it provides recognition.

These talks should be aimed at letting the employee know that we recognize him as a living human being—a person with a background, a family and interests in life. If we use people-empathy to hold these conversations, then we will do them in a less formal atmosphere. People-empathy will help us make the atmosphere more conducive to the employee talking with us. If we always try to hold these conversations in our office, the conversation may become one-sided and somewhat stilted. It is a well-known fact that a desk becomes a natural barrier between a manager and employees. Many managers who use people-empathy are rearranging their offices in order to avoid this situation. The desk is being placed against the wall with a more informal seating arrangement evolving. A round coffee table is excellent for this purpose.

It is also important that we should spend a small part of each day saying hello to our employees and giving them just a few minutes to tell us what might be on their minds. A good time for this is at the coffee break. When we manage with people-empathy, we realize that giving up a little bit of our time will pay important dividends in the future. Employees really appreciate managers who use people-empathy and "socialize" with them a little bit. The coffee break is a relaxed time; it is a good time to really get to know the employees, not the time to talk business. Rather, managers who use people-empathy find it an excellent time to talk about fishing, football games, baseball games, current events and whatever the employees feel like discussing. Sometimes our employees may have done something that is important to them and they would like to tell us about it. This may be difficult if we are busy, but the employee wants to tell us while the news is fresh. We must remember that this is important to the employee. Also, he must think well of us if he wants to tell us. By being willing to listen to our employees, we are recognizing them and are using people-empathy to become more effective managers.

HOW TOM S. HAD AN IDEA THAT PAID OFF IN RECOGNITION

Tom S. was personnel manager for an airline. Shortly after he had taken over his position, he decided to visit with all the employees and to see what some of their problems were. On his trip he noticed that the pilots, flight attendants, ground crews, mechanics, and ticket attendants had no concept of the management organization of the company. Because of the nature of the operation, most of them were isolated from their top management. He also noticed that top management tended to stay in the company headquarters location.

After returning from the field, Tom decided to set up a new indoctrination program with people-empathy. Each new employee, whether he was a pilot or a mechanic, would be flown to the company headquarters. There, he would be introduced to the top management of the company. He would be allowed to tour the headquarters and see what made the operation tick. He also made sure that the personnel already working for the company had this opportunity. This simple act done with people-empathy paid off by providing recognition for the employees of the airline. They felt like the top management of their company was recognizing them. The program was so successful that within 18 months, Tom S. was promoted to the position of corporate vice-president.

HOW TO SUCCESSFULLY USE YOUR COMPANY PUBLICATION FOR RECOGNITION

Many companies today have a company publication, usually a company newsletter or newspaper. However, the company publication is usually just that—a *company* publication. It is the medium by which the company tells the employee *it* is an outstanding company and therefore, the employees should like it.

The company publication is the means for the company to tell the employee how good the benefits are that it provides him. It also becomes an opportunity for the company to editorialize. This is the opportunity to explain the evils of absenteeism, overstaying breaks or for a change of pace, perhaps talking about problems associated with drugs. In many instances, the employees view this as preaching. It stimulates little interest of itself since most employees probably can discover the same information from more informative sources.

However, if we manage with people-empathy, then we realize that the company is more than a great, benevolent, inanimate object. The company consists of its employees. Therefore, it is a logical step to use people-empathy and recognize that a company publication should rightly be about, and for, the employees of the company. A good company publication produced with people-empathy contains many pictures of its employees and their families.

The company publication should be a means of recognizing the achievements made by the employees. Achievements are those things of which an employee is proud. These include such things as perfect attendance, length of service, or developing a suggestion that was used by the company. Whatever it is, the employee wants to be recognized. He appreciates being able to show his family and friends that he was recognized, and he is also proud that his fellow workers know of his achievement.

If we are managing with people-empathy, we know that the employees are interested in what other employees do. As a source of recognition we might feature a "Department of the Month," telling the purpose and goals of that department and what each of the employees in that department does to contribute to the success of the company. There are many departments in the company that employees know exist, but really don't know what they do. This is a golden opportunity to extend the contact between all workers. It will remove the veil of mystery that sometimes exists between production and service departments. When accomplished with people-empathy, this is an excellent form of recognition.

Another way we can recognize employees is by having an "Employee of the Month." This is a way of talking to our employees about other employees, and it gives the chosen employee a chance to be in the spotlight. By featuring an employee of the month, we can talk about someone who has an unusual hobby, who has done something outstanding for the company, or who has been an employee of the company for a long time and we are taking this opportunity to talk about him and his family. It is an excellent idea in managing with people-empathy to feature the employee's family with him. Many advanced companies call this feature the "Family of the Month" or "Meet Another Company Family." With people-empathy, we realize that our employees are interested in certain "newsy" items, such as weddings, births, and other unusual events external to the company. These should be included in the paper, but care must be taken to make sure that they don't dominate the entire issue. Also, some papers have been pleased with the success of a bulletin board feature in which employees may advertise items for "Swap and Shop."

To make such a publication successful and have it provide true recognition for our employees in the tradition of people-empathy, we should let the employees themselves contribute the most to the company publication. We will be pleasantly surprised to find that most employees can be truly creative in this respect. Because the company publication will be theirs, they will take an interest to make it a worthwhile medium for recognizing the employees. This also gives us another opportunity for recognition in that we can put a by-line with the article. Since all of us at one time or another have had the urge to write, we may find that some employees would like this opportunity to explore their creativity. On occasion, we might feature a story that has nothing to do with the company but is a means of displaying the creativity of some budding author. Such stories could be in the form of a short story or maybe a poem. In any event, the use of the company publication with people-empathy can provide a true source of recognition for our employees. All it takes is a little imagination.

HOW PHILLIP B. FOUND NEW WAYS TO RECOGNIZE HIS EMPLOYEES AND DISCOVERED THAT THEY CONTINUALLY IMPROVED IN PERFORMANCE

Phillip B. was the managing director of the local office of a state health facility. Under him were a staff of administrators and clerical personnel in addition to the usual complement of nurses. Everyone working under him was a specialist, so to speak, who had an important task to perform. Phillip managed with people-empathy. Phillip knew that, in general, people took it for granted that the health facility existed but were totally unaware of the contribution his employees made.

Phillip started providing his employees with recognition by using the State Health Department newspaper. Additionally, as his employees accomplished something, attended a training course, or for some other reason deserved recognition, he made sure a press release was issued to the local newspaper. He also made certain that this press release not only contained information regarding what the employee achieved, but also the background of his or her job. In this way he provided his employees with recognition and informed the town of the vital service provided by his employees. Whenever anyone from the state capitol visited his office for administration purposes, he made sure that they had an opportunity to meet each of his employees.

Because Phillip B. used people-empathy in providing his employees with recognition, he found that they continually strived to improve their performance. This was a source of motivation for his employees and he was recognized as being the most outstanding director of a local facility. Because of this, he was selected to serve on several prestigious committees.

HOW YOUR BOSS CAN HAVE A POSITIVE EFFECT ON YOUR EMPLOYEES BECAUSE OF EMPATHY

In many cases, an employee knows who his supervisor is, but he may be vaguely aware of his supervisor's superior. This usually results from one line of supervision separating the employee from the next higher supervisory level. The level above our supervisor then becomes something our employees may hear about from time to time. The "rules of the game" usually don't allow an employee the opportunity to jump these lines in order to have contact.

In facing facts, our supervisor may find that his time must be spent supervising those who report to him and dividing his attention among more important managerial duties. Unless the department is really small, chances are that in some instances our supervisor may not know the first names (or he may not be able to match the faces with the names) of our employees. We can provide our employees with recognition as well as helping our boss to manage with people-empathy if we follow these simple guidelines:

1. When an employee first comes to work for us, make sure that he meets our supervisor and receives an explanation of the job our supervisor does. He should also meet our supervisor's superior.
2. After the new employee has been on the job for about three or four weeks, he should spend approximately one hour with our supervisor talking about the function of the department and the employee's feelings at this time; in general, the time should be spent in getting to know each other.
3. Make sure that our boss gets around on a periodic basis to visit and talk with each of our employees, even if it is for five minutes.
4. Anytime our employees receive some form of award (service, attendance, etc.), have our boss make the presentation.

By meeting our supervisor on the first work day, the initial contact is made. It is obvious that any employee is going to be a little confused on the first work day. He isn't going to remember which drawer to put his lunch in, much less remember all about our boss; but our supervisor should have had an opportunity to learn something about the employee. Also, the employee will at least remember what the boss looks like and know that he does have something to do. This is an important step in managing with people-empathy. It should not be cast aside, nor should it be run through quickly and haphazardly. Any employee we feel should be hired by our company deserves the best.

Once the employee has been on the job long enough to get his bearings established, then it is time for another meeting with our supervisor. The time spent together at this meeting should be a minimum of one hour. Our supervisor should talk about his department, its goals and objectives and exactly where the employee fits in. This is sure to make an impression upon the employee as well it should; it is the opportunity for him to really get to know our supervisor. When we manage with people-empathy, we realize that this is time well spent. Our supervisor becomes a living, breathing person to whom our employee can relate. The employee must be encouraged to talk about his feelings, and this is a good time for him to ask questions that have been building for a time now. This is where managing with people-empathy can produce results capable of reaping big dividends in the future.

When our supervisor takes the time to occasionally visit and talk with our employees, it has a double benefit: first of all, the employees are kept aware of the fact that our boss really does exist; they feel that he is interested in them. These visits reinforce the sense of belonging in the employees. It gives them an opportunity to keep our supervisor up to date on the situation on a first-hand basis. Second, our supervisor gets to know our employees a little better. He gets to see for himself what the situation is, and he has the opportunity to tell the employees things they may ask about. Moreover, he gets the rare opportunity to do this from his point of view. When managing with people-empathy, we will find that this is important and the results achieved are astonishing.

An event that is important enough to merit an award is certainly to be considered an achievement. Therefore, we should feel that the occasion deserves the attention of our supervisor. By his presence, we make the event more meaningful for the employee. The only way we could improve upon this would be to have the highest ranking person in the company at our location present with our boss. This tells our employee that we sincerely recognize him and his achievements.

These simple steps will help make the employee feel that he is being recognized as part of the company. He will feel that someone higher than ourselves recognizes him and appreciates the job that he is doing. It will also impress upon the mind of the employee that managers do not live in "ivory towers," nor are they the ultimate in disciplinary measures. In other words, by managing with people-empathy we can recognize our employees and make them feel as if they belong.

HOW SINCERITY HELPED LEONARD J.

Leonard J. was the manufacturing manager for a company that produces toys. Leonard had been held back from promotion because of his inability to relate to others, particularly those a couple of levels below him. This problem had been pointed out to Leonard many times on his performance review, and finally he decided to do something about it. He decided to attend a course that was reportedly designed to improve personality and ability to relate to others.

Shortly after he had completed the course, things seemed to take a turn for the worse. His supervisor called him in for a talk. He pointed out to Leonard that now that he had attended this course, he was doing all of the things that he was supposed to be doing, but they were coming across insincerely as if Leonard was programmed to say those things.

Leonard's supervisor told him that he should manage with people-empathy. He pointed out that Leonard should have a sincere and honest desire to relate to the people around him and to his workers. Leonard thought about this and felt that he had nothing to lose by using people-empathy.

After six months of relating to his employees with sincerity and people-empathy, he was able to give them the recognition that they deserved. Because of this, his performance improved three times over, and within the next six months he was promoted to divisional general manager for his particular toy division.

HOW USING RECOGNITION CAN BE TO YOUR ADVANTAGE

Recognition is one of the tools of trade used by those who manage with people-empathy. It is a truly effective tool when used properly and with people-empathy. Recognition is one of the ways by which we can provide motivation for our employees; and when our employees are motivated, the results can be amazing. Motivated employees are productive employees. When they are motivated by recognition that is given through people-empathy, they feel that they belong and we recognize that they are employees with feelings.

If we manage with people-empathy, we realize that we need our ego inflated every now and then. However, true recognition does not merely inflate the ego for a short period of time. In a strict sense, recognition does not "inflate" the ego; rather it bolsters the entire person because it is sincere. The employee knows that he deserves the recognition. Recognition is an ongoing process when used with people-empathy. It is the means by which we can recognize an employee as being an integral part of the company, yet maintaining his individuality.

If we provide our employees with recognition through the use of people-empathy, we create an atmosphere in which they are willing to strive for the goals and objectives of their department and the company as a whole. By providing sincere, honest recognition with people-empathy, we will be able to see improvements in our department in a short period of time. If we already practice people-empathy and provide recognition for our employees, then we are fully aware of the advantages it offers. The results obtained through the use of people-empathy in giving recognition will certainly make our jobs as managers easier.

7

*How to Gain Employee
Support Painlessly When
Initiating Needed Change*

Change has created problems for people throughout history. But change is inevitable if progress is to be made. Now more than ever before, change is important if we are to meet the challenges that face us. We, and our employees, will have to adapt to new organizational concepts, machines, technical innovations, new jobs and many other ways of living in our environment. Change has been especially painful for managers to initiate. There is a two-fold reason for this: first of all, the manager must adapt to the change himself; and second, he anticipates an unfavorable reaction from his employees. It does not come easy to a manager to implement change. Change that has been initiated ineptly has resulted in many arbitration proceedings. Even though we all begin to feel comfortable with things the way they are, we will not only have to find ways of changing ourselves, but we must help our employees adapt to the change. This is necessary if we are to stay dynamic and productive. Through people-empathy, we will be able to help our employees welcome change.

WHY EMPLOYEES LIKE THE STATUS QUO

Anytime that we initiate a change that affects an employee, it involves a loss of security for him. This fear of the loss of security is very real for employees, and it is important that we recognize this fact. When we manage with people-empathy, we realize that our employees are no longer faced with the familiar, the routine, and those things which they have mastered. The environment that our employees have taken pains to cultivate and make comfortable will give way to change. With people-empathy we realize that our employees feel that they are facing something that is unpredictable. The environment surrounding them gives them a sense of identity. A teller in a bank develops a sense of security achieved from the identity of the job that he does. This is an important fact for our employees. When we manage with people-empathy, we recognize the need for the security of this identity in our employees.

Through the use of people-empathy we also realize that change can cause our employees to feel like they have lost status. The environment gives the employee a means of establishing a niche. Whenever we make a change, we upset the environment and leave the employee wondering about his status. With people-empathy, we realize that our employees constantly compare the job they do with the jobs that everyone else in the organization does. When we initiate a change, they lose the sense of comparison, at least for a time. Therefore, it is natural for them to feel that they have lost some level of status. Status may mean more than a social level; it can mean an orderly place in the organization. Also, when we manage with people-empathy we realize that a change can affect what employees' families, friends, and even co-workers think of them and their status.

People-empathy also helps us to realize that changes can cause our employees concern over economic conditions. After all, employees are involved in trying to make a living for their families. They will want to know how the change affects their seniority. Seniority provides an important sense of security for our employees. They also may wonder how the change will affect future pay increases. When we manage with people-empathy, we realize that when we make a change, employees will wonder who is obtaining what advantage over them. Sometimes, the economic situation may not be quite so evident, such as loss of shift premium, when we move an employee to the day shift. When the national economic conditions are not good, an employee may fear a move to a new job. When we manage with people-empathy, we recognize these fears.

In many instances when change is initiated, it usually winds up with the employee being changed rather than having him change according to current needs. Top management usually decides that a change is necessary and tells the employee that he has to do something different and expects him to accomplish the change. When we manage with people-empathy, we realize that the most effective means of accomplishing change is to have it initiated by the employees. This does not mean that we manipulate them into thinking it was their idea; rather, people-empathy demands that we be honest with our employees. But in order to implement change, we should let them participate and keep them thoroughly informed. We involve them in the decisions. We don't wait until the change is installed to bring our employees on board.

HOW JOYCE G. INSTITUTED CHANGE AND OVERCAME OBSOLESCENCE

Joyce G. was the director of a local municipal water works company. When Joyce took over the job, she did so through the usual seniority system. She was a dynamic supervisor with ideas that would move her department forward. It did not take Joyce long to realize that many of the activities for which she was responsible were initiated some 30 years ago. In any normal business these practices would have been deemed obsolete, and newer, more efficient practices would have been put into operation.

Joyce also knew that most of her employees had been around for many years. They had become set in their ways and any changes which she might want to initiate could create problems. She also knew that if she didn't begin making changes soon, the water works would be severely deficient in being able to keep up with the needs of a growing city.

Joyce was a manager who used people-empathy. Therefore, she did not assume that she knew all the answers necessary to make the changes. She also knew that people do not object to change as much as they object to being changed, so she called all her employees together for a meeting. Joyce explained the problems they were faced with in trying to make an outmoded system keep pace with a growing city. By talking to the employees and soliciting their ideas about modernizing the system, Joyce was able to involve them in the necessary changes.

Actually, the meetings produced ideas that Joyce had not even considered. Within three weeks they had installed one of the most modern systems of any water works. It wasn't long before many other municipalities were coming to study the system instituted by Joyce and her employees. As a result of the efficiencies gained by the system, the mayor and board of city commissioners were able to authorize a handsome increase as a bonus for Joyce.

HOW EMPATHY CAN HELP TO INITIATE NEW IDEAS—PAINLESSLY

We know that in any business or operation we will have to initiate new ideas if we are to be successful. When we manage with people-empathy it is easier for us to bring about new ideas and changes. We look to those aspects of managing with people-empathy that will best achieve the needed results. There are several things which we can do to operate with people-empathy.

1. As managers, we cannot take it for granted that we have considered all of the details involved in the change.
2. We as managers must realize that change can be a slow process.
3. We must give consideration to the effects of the change on all aspects of the job.
4. As much as possible, we should involve the workers in participating in and initiating the change.
5. We must explain the change to everyone in the organization even if they are not affected by it. This explanation should include the effects on those involved.

Although our position and experience gives us a good look at the "big picture," there are many details of the change we can overlook. These details can return to haunt us if we do not look after them. Therefore, if we manage with people-empathy, we know that we must look to those people who can help us fill in the details, and this must include our employees. They are close to the situation and can readily advise us on the small details of which we might be unaware. We should also look to the experts in the company's policies. Any changes could cause an impact on the policies, and we should have advice on the matter. In this way we can avoid violating policy or creating a situation that will make it difficult to implement the policy in the future when we might need it the most. If the change will have an impact on production activities, we should involve the industrial engineering department so that they can keep abreast of changes in their standards.

When we are thinking about making a change, it may not take very long for us to develop the recommendation; however, when it comes to implementing the change, time could come to a standstill. We may tend to lose our patience and take whatever action will cause us to get on with the change. When we manage with people-empathy, we recognize that change can be a very slow and time-consuming project. We also realize that by ramming the change through, we can do more harm than good. Therefore, we will take this time to perfect the components of the change. We monitor the change process and compare it to our plan, using this opportunity to look for ways to improve change. We work with the people involved so that they feel thoroughly comfortable with the change. We look for areas of possible misunderstanding so that we can keep them cleared up. In this way, by using people-empathy we can make this time work for us.

It is extremely important that we look at the effect of the change on all aspects of the job. When we manage with people-empathy we know that overlooking the effect of the change on a small part of the job can cause us problems in the long run. For instance, suppose we overlook the effect on seniority; we could be causing undue problems for our employees in the future. All aspects of the job include the impact on other jobs or departments. In using people-empathy, we make sure that everyone affected has been consulted.

When we make a change, we must explain it to everyone in the organization, even if they are not immediately affected by it. With people-empathy, we can see that our employees have a desire to know. When they are kept uninformed, they may draw their own conclusions. So keeping our employees informed prevents undue alarm or concern. In some instances, the announcement need not be detailed but should contain sufficient information as in the announcement of a promotion. In other instances, extremely detailed information may be needed as in the announcement of a promotion. In other instances, extremely detailed information may be needed as in the announcement of a cut-back in one department—all workers are certainly interested in how we handle this one.

If we follow these procedures, it will be a much less

difficult job for us to initiate change. We can effect change in a way that helps us accomplish the objective of the company. These principles which involve people-empathy help our people realize that they are changing with the needs of the company and are not *being changed*. Our employees become involved in the change rather than hearing about it through an obscure company announcement or through the grapevine. Through people-empathy we have access to many more resources.

HOW THE ARDEN COMPANY CHANGED ITS
SHIFT SCHEDULE PAINLESSLY

The Arden Company was a manufacturer of ladies apparel. They had not been in the industry long, but were experiencing a tremendous growth rate from their marketing activities. As a result of their growth, they had developed back orders of such a magnitude that it was going to require some changes to increase capacity. It would take them at least two years before they would be prepared with another plant to help increase capacity, so they were going to have to look elsewhere. The Arden Company had considered adding more people, but this would not help matters since they were limited by floor space to the number of machines currently in operation. After much consideration, it appeared that the only useful answer was to add a third shift.

Adding the third shift was not as easy as it seemed. It involved moving some of the more senior employees to a less desirable shift in order to adequately staff it with qualified personnel. Being a company that operated with people-empathy, the Arden Company called the employees together and began outlining the problems which they would face. They pointed out some of the alternatives that they had explored and the reasons for rejecting them. The management of the Arden Company approached the employees with the idea of a third shift and began soliciting ideas from them for making it work.

By the end of the meeting the Arden Company had arrived at a spectacular new shift arrangement that would increase production without adding a third shift.

It was rather complicated and basically involved two shifts of ten hours each for four days and two shifts of twelve hours each for three days. The various shifts would rotate through the schedule so that no one shift was subjected to hardships for any longer period than six weeks. As a result of this revolutionary new shift arrangement obtained through people-empathy, the Arden Company realized a 33% increase in production.

HOW SUPERVISORS CAN AVOID BUNGLING CHANGE

If we do not use people-empathy when we make a change, we leave opportunity for complications. When a change is necessary, a supervisor must do two things in order to avoid bungling the situation: first of all, he must realize that change cannot be accomplished overnight. Sometimes a situation is "easier said than done." What appears easy to us may be difficult for our employees to understand and implement. If we as supervisors operate with people-empathy, we realize that we must give consideration to the time element. The time element is important not only from the standpoint of planning but as an expectation in the minds of our employees. Many times we like to look at the optimistic side of a situation. Because of this, we may predict that a change can be implemented in the period of one month when in reality it may take as long as six months. We may overlook the training aspect, or perhaps lead-time in obtaining new equipment. Therefore, we must give consideration to the people-empathy portion of a change as much as the physical aspect of a change. In this way we can anticipate the needs of our employees. If anything, from the standpoint of people-empathy, we would be better off to overestimate the time needed to implement a change. In scheduling a change, we must set realistic goals; if we do not, we can doom the change to failure before we begin. This is not to say that the goal need not be challenging. Indeed, we must not set the goals so loosely as to be meaningless from a business standpoint. But our employees must feel that what is expected of them is reasonable. People-empathy helps us to do this.

The second point which we must keep in mind when using people-empathy to implement a change is the avoidance of putting pressure on our employees. In the past there has been a bias built into changes that prepared us for the worse. We all would realize, either consciously or subconsciously, that employees tend to resist change. We "knew" before we announced a change that we weren't going to be able to "sell" it. Therefore, it seemed that it was easier on us as managers if we took the attitude "do it or else." Of course, this took a particular type of personality to come down hard like this. Another way of accomplishing the same thing is when a supervisor approaches his employees and says that the top man in the company has ordered this change and that there is nothing that we can do about it but that we *must comply*. This takes the monkey off the supervisor's back but it still backs the employees up against the wall. They still come away with the same sense of frustration.

If we operate with people-empathy, we realize that the application of pressure is not the way to make change work. As a matter of fact, we realize that this can have just the reverse effect. When we manage with people-empathy, we realize that change requires a stronger interaction between us and our employees. We must actively involve our employees so that they will cooperate to the fullest to make the change work. With people-empathy, we realize that for change to be effective it must be accomplished harmoniously. With people-empathy, we help make it easy for our employees to pull in the same direction as we are pulling. The change then becomes much more meaningful.

HOW TIM A. GOT HIS EMPLOYEES TO AGREE TO A MAJOR CHANGE WITHOUT ANY COMPLAINTS

Tim A. was the manager of a large department store. During his frequent trips through the store, Tim noticed that it was taking a considerable amount of time for his clerks to conclude a sale. He realized that the problem centered around a bottleneck created by the cash registers and the old machines for charge plates. Through investigation, he found that there was a computerized system that could reduce this time by as much as one-half.

Being a manager who used people-empathy, Tim decided not to make the change until he could involve his employees. Tim talked to each of his employees and explained the problem and his proposed solution. He also proposed that over the period of the next two months he would send each of his employees to the vendor for indoctrination into the system and for their evaluation. So that his employees would not all be out of the store at the same time, he sent them on a rotating schedule.

After the employees returned from their indoctrination session, they were asked to evaluate the system thoroughly and give their input as to ways in which they could improve upon it. After the employees had all been through the indoctrination at the vendor location and the evaluations were in, Tim began implementing this system, one department at a time.

As each system was installed, all employees were invited to spend some time in the department going over the techniques to be used and to ensure that everyone was in accord with what was expected. As a result of using people-empathy, Tim implemented a major change without a single complaint. The savings to the store came much faster than expected, and top management rewarded Tim handsomely at year end with a significant bonus.

HOW SUPERVISORS CAN FACILITATE
CHANGE THROUGH EMPATHY

We need not force each change with trepidation, but we can look to it as a means of moving onward and upward. If we use people-empathy, then we realize that there are several things that we as managers can do to help make the change easier. These principles can be summarized as follows:

1. Thoroughly explain the change, as well as the need for the change, to the employees involved.
2. Involve those who will be significantly affected by the change.
3. Consult with the employees who are involved in the change.
4. Handle each situation of change separately and distinctly from any other situation.

When we make change, it is necessary to use people-empathy and realize that those who will participate in the change need to know what it is all about. There are many aspects of this to be viewed by the employee. One of the first things that we must do in telling our employees about the change is to explain what is in it for them. If an employee feels we are exploiting him, he will be less likely to help make the change work. Also, the employee must know what is expected of him. He will need to know the new procedure, and he must know what new policies will be put into effect. We must use people-empathy and look at the change from the point of view of the employee. Then we explain the change to him from this point of view. With people-empathy we can be sure that our employees understand the change and can now help make it succeed.

The employee is smart and he realizes that the change is of benefit to top management in the company. We do not need to explain this part of the change to him. While explaining, we also need to maintain our credibility. This is vitally important. With people-empathy, we realize that by overselling the benefits and underselling the negative aspects of the change, we can create credibility gaps which can seriously affect future change. Therefore, we should strive to explain the change as it is. With people-empathy we realize that we also must explain the negative aspects of the change as well as the positive. By explaining the negative as well as positive aspects, we will be demonstrating to our employees that we have looked at the situation from all viewpoints. We can then show that the positive aspects outweigh the negative and that it is of benefit to proceed with the change. When we do not explain all points of view, our employees are liable to feel that we have something to hide. When we are honest with people-empathy, the results will be the painless initiation of change.

Additionally, we know that we must explain the change far enough in advance for the employees to be able to evaluate its effect on them. Our employees are like us—they like to have time to think about the change and its overall results. When we operate with people-empathy we realize that we must eliminate the element of surprise. If we spring a change on an employee, he does not feel a part of the change. He does not have a chance to digest the ramifications of the change, nor will he be disposed to help us implement the change. An employee given ample time to consider the change will react much more favorably than one who is told just prior to the impending change.

One of the surest ways to implement change painlessly is to involve our employees. The employees become a part of the change and not people who have been changed. Tim A. used people-empathy in this manner when he had his sales clerks attend the indoctrination session and evaluate the new computerized system. The change may not always involve sending employees to a vendor, but in many instances they are the true experts in their day-to-day activities. By involving them in the change, we may not only have employees more willing to change, but we may obtain ideas not considered. Our employees know their jobs so intimately that they can see things we may overlook. Their ideas may be more sound, so they can make recommendations that might improve the original concept. We certainly will allow the change to be implemented more satisfactorily. This means that we consult with them in the early stages of the idea that will produce the change. We must not wait until we are ready to announce the change to involve the employees.

In many phases of the operation of our business, we have employees who are experts in that particular area of the operation. This is precisely why we hired them for the purpose of advising us on their areas of expertise. Therefore, if we operate with people-empathy, it would seem natural that we should consult with them in making the change. This also can serve to give us an outside view of the change. They will be more aware of the pitfalls that need to be avoided than we. Many times they can look at the change from an unbiased viewpoint. People-empathy also tells us that they, being the experts, are often looked up to by other employees and they can help us facilitate the change. These experts can be company-trained experts who have moved ahead based on their ability to analyze situations and understand our process. In some instances, the workers themselves may be more tuned to the process than the company engineers. After all, they do the task on a daily basis. Therefore, we should include knowledgeable employees in the consultation as well as the company experts. When we manage with people-empathy, we realize that we do not have to "go it alone."

HOW STEVE C. ACHIEVED CHANGE
AND WON A PROMOTION

Steve C. was general superintendent in a company that manufactures specialty gears. Steve had come from the "old school" that maintained that when the general superintendent said do something, that meant the employees were to do it immediately with no questions asked. However, over the past several months, he noticed that the employees were reacting less favorably to this method of supervision. During some of the conversations he had with a friend in whom he could confide, he began learning about people-empathy. It was hard for him to accept that managing with people-empathy could work. He could not shake the feeling that employees ought to do something because he, the general superintendent, said to do it. However, he was faced with a major change that would ultimately result in redistribution of his labor force. This was one opportunity which he could not afford to have go sour, so he decided to use people-empathy.

Using the principles of accomplishing change through people-empathy, Steve began. Six months before the change was to occur, he talked to all the employees explaining the reasons for the change and how it would affect them. He began meeting with those employees who would be involved in the change. Together they drafted up the policies, the transfer of seniority, established new job descriptions, and in general took care of many of the aspects that Steve would probably have overlooked. In many instances, he might have accomplished this change with token consultation with the industrial engineering department and perhaps the personnel department; however, he not only involved these departments but the employees themselves. When the time for the change came, everything moved smoothly and much more quickly than anticipated. The results were so effective and so impressed top management that Steve C. was promoted to plant manager with a substantial increase in his paycheck.

HOW TO ACHIEVE CHANGE PAINLESSLY

If we are to achieve change painlessly, we must use people-empathy. We must realize that people really don't mind change as much as they mind *being* changed. Our employees are as interested in the success of the company as we are. People are not really interested in perpetuating obsolete methods; they simply feel a sense of security in the things that they have been doing. But they are more than willing to change if we approach the change with people-empathy. We must also recognize through people-empathy that because of our past practices, employees sometimes become suspicious that change is being made for the benefit of management at their expense. This is a tough point for us to overcome. The principal ingredient in accomplishing change through people-empathy is the involvement of the employee.

Further, if we wish to initiate change painlessly, there is one element which must not be overlooked—the supervisor. The supervisor interfaces daily with the employees. He represents the company to them, but he also represents the employees. If our employees sense that their supervisor is not happy about the change, no amount of activity on our part can convince them otherwise (unless the supervisor is totally disliked by the employees). Therefore, we must not bypass our supervisors but we must thoroughly involve them. We must consider them in their roles of supervisors and also in their roles of employees. As a matter of fact, the best agent of change that we can use is the supervisor himself. Principles of initiating change apply to supervisors as well as to employees. Therefore, involvement of the supervisor with people-empathy can go a very long way toward ensuring success of a much needed change.

Another important aspect of implementing change is our own viewpoint. If we decide that we are going to make a change and then close our minds from that point on, we could be headed for severe difficulties. When we manage with people-empathy, we must keep our minds open. We may feel that we have weighed all the pros and cons and determined that the good outweighs the bad, but we can be wrong. By looking at the situation with people-empathy, we keep an open mind and look at other points of view. This helps us minimize the risk of a bad decision. We are also willing to admit that maybe this change we had in mind is not necessary after all.

In many instances, we need not even decide what change is needed. After we have properly determined that a change is necessary, our employees and the company experts can help us formulate the change that will accomplish our objective. But we must serve as resource persons who can provide the needed inputs for a sound decision. With people-empathy, these aspects of management become much easier to accomplish.

8

Understanding Employee Needs, Emotions and Personalities Through People-Empathy

When we talk to people, we bring into play several elements of human behavior. We engage in actions and reactions, and we make assumptions. There are different meanings attached to words. We have needs to be satisfied; we express emotions which affect our point of view, or the point of view of those with whom we are communicating.

Each of us has a need to know and understand. When denied complete knowledge about a matter that concerns us, we rationalize. We make patterns out of isolated events, and we draw conclusions. Therefore, it is important that we communicate completely and timely. By satisfying the need to know in each of our employees, we can help them avoid rationalizing. With people-empathy, we can avoid creating a breakdown in understanding.

Efforts to communicate effectively are often directed toward the mistaken belief that "if at first you don't succeed, overwhelm them with information." Many times the form of communication is mistaken for its substance. Sometimes we go astray when we consider communication as a simple, isolated event. When we manage with people-empathy, we realize that communicating is a complex and dynamic process, and we place our emphasis on the entire process. This will help lead to a complete understanding. Many times we emphasize the wrong part of communicating and understanding. A boss might decide that his organization isn't communicating effectively; he might send all of his managers to a course on business writing. Their correspondence might get better, but it is doubtful that communications will improve.

Sometimes we communicate outcomes so that even if we are not right all the time, we are never wrong. This is using a "safety valve," and we are using "weasel words." But this is not managing with people-empathy. Therefore, it does not help our supervision become painless. Usually, if an outcome is not what we anticipated within certain limits of expectation, we feel frustrated. Therefore, our communications sometimes tend to be vague, which can lead to a breakdown in understanding. By the proper use of people-empathy we can overcome this tendency and avoid the possibility of a breakdown in understanding.

If we manage with people-empathy, we will not let our communications be incomplete. Often, we do not like to tell everything because we might be admitting our weaknesses. To tell every detail would be tedious for us and boring for our audience. Then, too, we may not remember all the facts exactly as they occurred; and as a result, we communicate incomplete or shaded information. This is a fact of life that exists in all of us. We ourselves may make every effort to communicate complete facts whenever possible, but those who are communicating with us may not be aware of this need. Therefore, people-empathy tells us that we must be aware of this difficulty in communicating that exists in all of us. By being aware of this problem, we can develop a stronger sense of understanding between us and our workers and make our jobs of supervising others that much easier.

HOW BOB O. SPOTTED A PROBLEM
AND SAVED $10,000

Bob O. ran a good maintenance operation. He noticed that on occasion when his workers were tackling a particularly frustrating job, their emotions began to rise and communications began to decline. He even noticed the same fact among his supervisors. On one occasion when his employees were working on a critical shaft and the shaft broke, the employees involved became emotional over the situation. One of them suggested that they call Bob to see if he might have ideas for salvaging the shaft; but before calling him, the other wanted to know what Bob could do. The first employee tried to tell the other that the reason for calling Bob was to see if he might have some suggestions. "If I knew what ideas he might have, then I could fix the shaft myself," the other replied. This line of reasoning was not producing results because of the emotional state that existed. Several minutes were spent in discussion. Bob was finally called and the shaft was salvaged; however, he was called for help out of frustration and not as the result of the logic of any suggestion. It was obvious that attempts to communicate were not successful. When communications were needed, the channels were not successful. When communications were needed, the channels were blocked by emotions.

Bob O. reflected on this and came up with a practical solution. In the future, when any of the employees were tackling a particularly frustrating job and a disagreement arose, they were to take a coffee break. However, the employees were to take another employee or one of the supervisors with them for the purpose of discussing the problem and developing a course of action that would lead to solutions. During the next year, this painless approach enabled Bob's department to realize a cost savings of $10,000 in suggestions made by his employees over these "coffee breaks."

By developing people-empathy, Bob O. helped create an atmosphere of understanding in his department. Through this understanding, he made his supervision painless. By looking for ways in which we can develop understanding with our employees, we increase the possibilities for improving performance and making our supervision painless.

HOW OVERCOMING LANGUAGE BARRIERS MAKES SUPERVISION EASIER

The world around us is made up of a great variety of values. These values hardly exist as black and white; rather, they are composed of an infinite number of shades of gray. These values form our concepts of the environment in which our relations to one another exist. Language is necessary to represent these concepts, but it can be misleading because it is bound by a rigid structure that forces us to view the world as if it is made up of absolutes. Because of this fact, people-empathy is required to avoid misunderstandings and subsequent breakdowns in communication.

Language is the medium by which we transmit ideas and information. Our language has progressed to the point that it contains many words, most of which have more than one definition. Through people-empathy we realize that the relationship between words and their definitions of the moment depends upon the intention of the user. The use of our language has been extended beyond the simplicity of the single bits of information contained in the original roots of our words. Hence, many of our common words are filled with potential ambiguity.

When we try to communicate, we should use people-empathy and compare our definitions to the concept we are discussing. If we truly have people-empathy, then we will take the time, in advance, to decide on our definitions for the central concepts of a conversation. This will keep us from blundering along only to find, to our frustration, that our language has become an ineffective medium for communications.

We often forget that in order for someone to understand us, that person must know our purpose in using the words we do and our definition of those words. This holds true for most of our nontechnical words which can have a vast range of meanings. In addition to the standard definitions, there are regional and vocational variations in the use of words. New words are being developed; and established words develop new meanings, or lose old ones.

Since communication involves a sender and a receiver, there are at least two meanings applied to the words used: the implied meaning, and the inferred meaning. If the two meanings are approximately the same, then good understanding will be the result. If the two meanings are not the same, then a breakdown can occur. People-empathy is a painless way of ensuring that the two meanings are approximately the same. With people-empathy we will realize the difficulties others are having in trying to understand our definition of the words, whether we are the senders or the receivers.

When we communicate, we are imparting a meaning from one person to another; and because of this, our meanings are subjective. Our emotions affect our understanding. We communicate our interpretation of reality instead of reality itself. When a sender's and a receiver's perception of the symbols that represent this reality are close together, understanding is easier.

We communicate by using symbols, devices that are designed to suggest certain meanings. We do not transmit meanings; we transmit symbols and the receiver then subjectively takes meaning from these symbols. The exchange of words is a personal, human process. People-empathy enables us to realize that the meaning which a receiver takes depends upon his experience and attitude—not the transmitter's. The transmitter only determines the intended meaning. This is an important concept in developing empathy in communicating.

Suppose a supervisor drives up in a hurry and on the way to his office yells at one of his men, "Tommy, how about taking the battery out of my car and putting it in the delivery truck in place of the one that went dead this morning." What do you think Tommy is going to do? Do you think he will take the battery out of the back seat of the supervisor's car unless he accidentally sees it there?

The meaning which Tommy takes depends on his experience, not on what the supervisor means. In order for our understanding to be complete, we need empathy to give major emphasis to the concept that transfer of meaning is aided by addressing communication in terms of the experiences and attitudes of the receiver.

Effective use of words does not mean correct grammatical structure. It is the ability to use people-empathy to transfer to others the meaning we intend. Words are important because we not only talk with them, we think with them. Since words have no certain meanings, we can make sense only through context. We use a word within a certain environment and we surround that word with other words until we narrow the meaning to the limits we desire. In order to have effective understanding, we must use people-empathy to concentrate on ideas and concepts rather than words. We must develop people-empathy so that we place our words in the proper environment and narrow the meaning to the limits of understanding.

In order to develop effective understanding, the receiver must react to words as the transmitter intended him to react. In other words, the receiver must translate the words into a meaningful concept. This translation must be done with people-empathy in order to correspond to the meaning the transmitter intended, or a breakdown occurs.

If we have people-empathy when we use words to make up sentences or paragraphs, then they will be as concrete as possible. This holds true whether the words are spoken or written. In order for words to be concrete, they should point at what they stand for. If we say, for example, "This bracelet costs

$3.00," then we are being more concrete than if we say, "This bracelet is inexpensive."

When we use concrete words, we help develop understanding. The word *chair* is concrete, but it can mean any chair at all. The more we use people-empathy, the more we can say about the chair and the more we set it apart from other chairs. The more specific we get about this chair, the more characteristics we give it. Certainly we are being more specific if we say, "the mahogany rocking chair" instead of "the rocking chair."

A good rule for effective understanding is to communicate with people-empathy and use concrete and specific words. Concrete, specific language is clear language. As a general rule, the communicator should use words that he knows his intended audience understands. To make sure that our listener understands our communication, we should use simple words. If we say that a person is wise, most everyone would understand what we meant. If we say that a person is cogent, there would be some people who might not know what we meant. Simple words should be short and clear.

Concrete, specific words can be simple words, but this is not always true. *Conflagration* is concrete, but not simple. We would be understood better if we said *fire*. So, in addition to being concrete and specific, words should also be simple.

HOW MARTY M. "LEARNED THE LINGO" AND EARNED A SUBSTANTIAL SALARY INCREASE

Marty M. was recently hired by an East Tennessee manufacturing firm as a front line supervisor. He was considered to be a bright individual with a promising future. With a few years of experience behind him, he seemed to have the potential to move up in the management ranks.

Not long after Marty joined his company, he needed to have one of his employees come in on Saturday and work overtime in order to get some shipments out. When he approached this employee and made his inquiries, Marty received the following reply: "I don't care to work on Saturday." Needless to say, such a response took him by surprise; however, it was to his credit that he did not react immediately to the problem. He backed off from the situation and decided to review the problem during the next week until he could get a handle on what this seeming insubordination meant. In the meantime, he found another employee who only said "Okay."

The following week when Marty approached another employee about working on Saturday he again got the response, "I don't care to work on Saturday." He again withdrew from the situation long enough to have a friendly discussion with his plant manager seeking advice on what to do.

The plant manager was a native of East Tennessee and understood the problem immediately. He explained to Marty that there were geographical meanings to phrases being used. He explained that when an employee says, "I don't care to," he is really saying in effect, "I don't mind . . . . . " Marty then took this opportunity to sit down and analyze the situation and realized that when talking to his workers, it was highly important for him as a supervisor to fully understand the meanings they had for phrases, sentences or words. He realized that by using people-empathy and "learning the lingo," he could effectively find the key to understanding his employees. He wanted to be a top-notch supervisor; therefore, it was necessary for him to understand his employees and for them to understand him. It was through this incident that Marty developed the people-empathy necessary for him to become the key supervisor in his work force and to earn a substantial increase in salary.

DETECTING NONVERBAL MESSAGES CAN HELP OBTAIN RESULTS

Besides listening to the person with whom you are communicating in an attempt to learn his desires and needs, you must also closely observe his gestures with people-empathy. For example, in a friendly conversation if someone suddenly sits back and folds his arms with abruptness, you would know at once that trouble has arrived.

Gestures are tremendously important. They convey many shades of meaning and have their psychological undertones and overtones. Therefore, if we wish to develop empathy to assist in understanding, we should continually observe the gestures of those with whom we are communicating in order to gain a clue to their thinking.

The term "gesture" is being used in the broadest possible sense; it includes much more than simple body motions. Tension can be shown by any number of signs such as blushing, contraction of facial muscles, fidgeting, undue preoccupation, strained laughter or giggling, or even just staring in silence. Actually, these are nonverbal means of communication.

Coughing frequently can have many implications. In some instances it has proved to be a form of nervousness, something the speaker depends on to help him go on talking. Often it is used to cover up a lie, or it may serve to express doubt or surprise on the part of the listener if someone talks about himself with too much confidence or conceit.

Facial expressions are obvious means of nonverbal communication, but the "poker face" confronts us with a total lack of expression, a blank look. This very lack of expression tells us that a man does not want us to know anything about his feelings. In spite of the assumed mask, we can read his intent.

Blinking is a protective reflex action to keep the eyes moist and to remove accumulated dust particles. However, studies have shown that the rate of blinking is higher when we are angry or excited. Normal blinking is hardly noticeable, but when it becomes a mannerism it attracts our attention by its frequency and repetition. In this abnormal state, blinking has been found to be connected with feelings of guilt and fear. It is used to hide something, and some research indicates that excessive blinking can serve as a lie detector. F. Lee Bailey tells the story of an overzealous judge who was aware of this fact and proceeded to instruct the jury by telling them that anyone can see that the defendant is guilty because of his excessive blinking. Of course, the defense attorney won his appeal because of that statement.

No matter how closely we observe with our eyes, however, we cannot completely gauge the emotional state of the person with whom we are communicating. Nevertheless, we must use people-empathy so that we can always be aware of the emotions lurking in the background whenever two or more people meet and talk.

The factors that affect emotions may be intangible. The room and setting in which a discussion is held can have an effect on the emotions of the conversation. It has been pointed out that discussions held in cheerful, brightly colored rooms are more successful and complete. The arrangement, location and details of decoration can have an important influence on understanding and must be viewed with people-empathy.

Aside from the surroundings, we can learn something by observing the way people move about during the discussion. If a person is interested in what is being said, he will lean forward and become a part of the conversation. The moment he loses interest, he will withdraw or back away.

Silent actions, gestures and movements of all kinds have something to tell if we can read them correctly. In a situation where we want people to look to us as a person of authority, we should try to sit at the head of the table. If we really want to develop people-empathy, we should try to sit on the side of the table with those who differ with us or our group and opinion. Then we attempt to take issue with certain propositions by our group, siding with those who differ. In minor things this appears to work because the differing group begins to consider us as a member of the team. Thereafter, they will listen most agreeably to our proposals for solving points of disagreement.

People can communicate different types of information at different levels of understanding. The communication process consists of more than the spoken or written language. In trying to communicate with a person, sometimes we get through and sometimes we do not—not because of what we said, or how we said it, or the logic of our thoughts, but because many times the reception of our communication is based upon the degree of the listener's empathy for our nonverbal communication.

A lover turning his back on his sweetheart and slamming the front door without a word is transmitting a significant message. It is, therefore, not difficult to understand how a person can develop people-empathy from understanding non-verbal language. Our emotional relations, mannerisms, habits and gestures are separate and distinct from those of a person sitting next to us at any social or business function, in our travels, or even members of our own family. Dealing with people by lumping them into one category or another runs the risk of creating more problems than it solves.

Feedback plays a major role in the full communication-with-empathy process, and gesture-clusters are important feed-back. They indicate from moment to moment, and movement to movement, exactly how individuals or groups are reacting nonverbally. We can learn whether what we are saying is being received in a positive manner or a negative one, whether the audience is open or defensive, self-controlled or bored. Speakers call this audience awareness, or relating to a group. Nonverbal feedback can warn you that you must change, withdraw or do something different to bring about the result that you desire. If we are *not* aware of feedback, there is a strong possibility that we will fail to communicate our believability, sincerity, or people-empathy to an individual or an audience.

An attorney was discussing the benefits he had derived from consciously considering nonverbal communications. He said that during the course of an office visit his client crossed his arms and legs "in a defensive position" and proceeded to spend the next hour admonishing him. Noticing the nonverbal implications of the client's gestures, he let his client talk it out of his system. Only after this did the lawyer offer professional advice on how to handle the difficult situation in which the client found himself. The attorney stated that had he not been grounded in nonverbal communication, he would not have given this client a chance to be receptive to him since he would not have read his client's needs and would probably have attempted to give him unheeded advice immediately.

HOW RECOGNIZING NEEDS AND EMOTIONS
LEADS TO EMPATHY IN SUPERVISION

Occasionally all parents have found that they must provide encouragement in one form or another to get their children to brush their teeth. Likewise, I was trying to convince my young daughter that she should brush her teeth. I told her that if she didn't brush her teeth, she wouldn't look pretty. Although she likes to be told she is pretty, my daughter wasn't reacting to this argument. She stood fast on her position that she wasn't going to brush her teeth.

I decided to change my tactics. I told her that if she didn't brush her teeth, little bugs in her mouth would eat holes in her teeth and they might even fall out. She took her toothbrush and began brushing vigorously.

A.H. Maslow developed a hierarchy of human needs, placed on a scale based on their urgency of satisfaction as motivators of behavior. On his scale, Maslow determined that the lowest (basic) needs must be satisfied before man will seek to satisfy the next need in the hierarchy. Once the lower need has been satisfied it ceases to be a motivator of behavior, and the individual then turns to the satisfaction of successively higher levels of needs.

Apparently my daughter knew what "pretty" was, but being so young some of her more basic needs were not yet satisfied in her mind. "Pretty" was at a level too high for her to understand and my communication failed. When I talked about the damage that could be done to the teeth, I was communicating on a more basic level and the communication was effective.

Each of us has a personality which becomes involved in our communications. This personality determines how our needs and emotions become involved. It is a process of change; specifically, it is the instrument of human psychological growth and development. In a real sense, a personality is who we are.

Through the process of genetics and heredity we are supplied with the basic equipment for survival and growth. This includes such physiological factors as body type, muscular and nervous systems, and the glands. We are also equipped by heredity with a basic intellectual capacity; however, the ways in which intelligence manifests itself in later life are more a function of environment.

Other constitutional factors which are determinants of personality include reduction of the basic drives such as hunger, thirst and sex. These urges and others like them may be satisfied in many ways which are determined more by our social culture than the primitive urge itself. There are elements of personality into which we can be categorized: *introvert* and *extrovert*. This implies that these are extremes, but it also includes the middle range between pure introvert and pure extrovert. It is important that we look at the difference between introvert and extrovert because the behavioral patterns of each can affect our understanding and are necessary before we can have empathy.

Most of us are aware of the basic difference between an introvert and an extrovert. We usually picture the introvert as being the mousey little man who sits in a corner too shy to come out and join the fun. On the other extreme, we see the extrovert as the happy-go-lucky salesman who is always the life of the party. This vaguely describes the extremes, but more is involved. As a matter of fact, approximately two-thirds of us are in the introvert range of the scale of personalities.

Psychologists have developed a test for determining if a person is an introvert or extrovert. It scores the answers from 1 to 100. If the score falls between 1 and 40, the person is considered to be an introvert. If the score is between 60 and 100, the person is considered an extrovert. Between 40 and 60, the person is a combination of the two.

Contrary to popular belief, opposites do not attract. For instance, a highly introverted man will usually not marry (at least not happily marry) a highly extroverted woman, or vice versa. Results from people who have taken this test indicate that a husband and wife will usually not vary more than five points between their scores. Although they each have certain traits in their own personality that complement an opposite trait in the partner's personality, on the whole their personalities are the same with regard to being an introvert or an extrovert.

Introverts tend to seek highly technical jobs requiring attention to detail. They make good lab technicians, book-keepers, clock and watch repairmen, and machine operators. Extroverts make good salesmen, public relations men, politicians and lawyers. An introvert is highly meticulous about housekeeping and regards the machine he operates as his and may actually resent others operating that machine. Above all, he resents being treated as an *extrovert*. He does not appreciate intrusions into his privacy and would prefer not being drawn out to participate on the same level as the extrovert.

On the other hand, extroverts would prefer to skim over the details and get at the heart of the matter. Their motto might be expressed like this: "Don't bother me with the labor pains, just show me the baby." They enjoy being the center of attention. Moreover, it does not bother an *extrovert* to be treated as an *introvert*.

Right away we can see that if we assume that everyone is an introvert (we would be right two-thirds of the time), our understanding and empathy would become more effective. By communicating on the level of the introvert, we will not offend the extrovert, we certainly won't offend the introvert, and we can develop a lot of empathy.

A story is told of a company controller. This gentleman

ran his accounting department on a highly efficient basis. However, most of the other department heads had a difficult time communicating with him. They would ask for reports and usually would have to wait several days for them. When they went into the weekly staff meetings, they would try to "butter him up." They would compliment him on the great game he bowled for the company team the night before.

The controller was an excellent bowler and had won many tournaments, but the high scores his co-workers complimented him on were average for him so these praises failed to impress him. He would usually clear his throat, but otherwise ignore these employees. His fellow workers could not succeed in establishing effective communication with him.

A new young man was brought into the organization and appointed Manager of Product Development. Being new, he arrived early for his first meeting. The controller was already there arranging his notes. Upon seeing the controller, the young man said, "Say Tom, I was driving past your house yesterday and I noticed that you like to sculpture animals in your hedges. I'm an amateur gardener myself and I'd like to stop by and have you show me your technique." The controller replied, "Why, I'd be delighted. How about stopping by this weekend?" After the staff meeting, the controller came over to the young man and said, "By the way, those reports you wanted by ten in the morning—well, I think I can have them on your desk by three this afternoon."

Obviously the controller was to the introvert side on the scale of personality. He was smart and could see through his fellow worker's attempts to "snow" him. His bowling scores were the same week after week, and he didn't feel it necessary to be complimented about them. However, his artistic accomplishments with the hedges were unusual; few people recognized his talent in this area. The one man who did was sincere in his efforts and satisfied the controller's need to be complimented in an area where he wanted recognition. The new Manager of Product Development made effective use of empathy.

Emotions can present a barrier to effective understanding. Suppose a supervisor and a worker have already had words over safety precautions. Now a change in product requires the supervisor to explain changes in precautions to all the employees in his department. Thirty workers assemble in a corner of the shop, and the supervisor begins to explain the new procedures. The disgruntled worker detests the supervisor, is convinced that nothing the supervisor says is worth hearing, and resents having to be there. The supervisor says, "After tomorrow we will be using an inflammable solvent." The worker isn't listening at all to what his supervisor is saying. He is muttering to himself, "Yeah you big lug, where do you get that 'we' stuff?" The worker doesn't get a word of what he is being told.

We are all more or less emotional; all of us are susceptible to *signal reaction,* that is, in some situations certain words or attitudes can provoke us into a nonrational response. So can annoyances, especially when repeated or prolonged. This often happens with colleagues, with superiors, with members of our families, with friends; and it happens with subordinates.

Such conditions and situations are too familiar to all of us. What we do not sufficiently realize is that these conditions must actually be changed before we can communicate and develop understanding and empathy. An attitude that *makes* understanding possible is necessary before understanding *is* possible— it's as simple as that. Yelling, self-rightousness and going about telling everyone how pig-headed the other fellow is do not facilitate empathy. But if there is sufficient basis for us to want to understand one another, we can get over these crises and communication once again becomes effective.

Other emotions can create problems in communication— the joy of a new baby in the family; the unhappiness of a quarrel with one's spouse; the sorrow of losing a loved one; the emotional strain of the job itself. Each of these situations creates a mood for the individual that can affect the reception of communication. As managers, we must be aware of these emotional filters and take positive steps to go beyond them and ensure that we have created empathy.

HOW KYLE LEARNED TO RECOGNIZE
NEEDS AND EMOTIONS AND BECAME
HIS COMPANY'S BEST SUPERVISOR

Kyle was an industrial engineering supervisor for a large mid-western company. He had several industrial engineers and technicians reporting to him. The company paid good wages and salaries and had the best benefits of any company in the area. This fact had been constantly preached to the supervisors and managers, and they were expected to bring the message to the workers.

Kyle periodically noticed that his employees referred to the company in less than complimentary terms. On occasions such as these, he took the opportunity to tell them about how the company pays good wages and salaries and has good benefits. However, he was told, "Yeah, but what has the company done for us lately? Nobody listens to us or cares about our problems!" Kyle came to realize that some of these complaints were symptomatic of the desire to have certain needs filled. After thoroughly analyzing the situation and investigating the theory behind Maslow's hierarchy of needs, Kyle began a departmental development program. As this program took shape, he began practicing participative management to its fullest. His own department was organized into specialty teams that comprised the whole Industrial Engineering department. His workers were participating in the decisions that affected them.

Kyle's department became one of the most effective departments in the company. It was highly productive and managed to do more work than any industrial engineering department in other divisions. This included some of the older and more sophisticated divisions in the company. Kyle had managed to satisfy the love and belonging needs of his workers. Through learning about the needs and emotions of the workers in his department, he became the most successful supervisor in the company and within two years he was promoted to the

Corporate Manager of Engineering with full responsibility for all industrial engineering departments.

HOW SUPERVISORS CAN
NEGOTIATE—PAINLESSLY

Life has been characterized as a series of negotiations. Supervisors constantly negotiate with their employees and with their fellow supervisors. The form may not assume the atmosphere and color of a full blown contract negotiation, but all the elements are there just the same. *In a successful negotiation everybody wins.*

Negotiating has often been compared with a game. A game has definite rules and a known set of values. Each player is limited in the moves he can make, the things he can and cannot do. True, some games have a greater element of chance than others, but in every game a set of rules governs the behavior of the players and enumerates their gains and losses. In games the rules show the risks and rewards; however, rules of this sort are not available in the unbounded life process of negotiation. In negotiating, any risks that are known have been learned from broad experience, not from a rule book. In a life situation, the negotiator ordinarily has little or no control over the complex variables, the innumerable strategies, that the opposer may bring into the struggle. Even more difficult is to know the value structure on which the opposer bases his strategy.

To look upon negotiating as a game to be played is to enter into the bargaining in a purely competitive spirit. With this attitude, the negotiator strives against other individuals for a goal which he alone hopes to attain. Even if he could persuade an opposer to "play" such a negotiating game, he would run the risk of being the absolute loser rather than the winner. In post-World War II Japan, some businessmen required their employees to study military strategy and tactics as a guide to successful business operations.

The objectives of negotiation should be to achieve agreement, not total victory. Both parties must feel that they have gained something. Even if one side had to give up a great deal, the overall picture is one of gain.

Negotiation, then, is not a game—and it is not war. Its goal is not a dead competitor. A negotiator ignores this point at his own peril. A person entering negotiation without empathy runs the risk of ignoring this point.

The cooperative approach to negotiation—the approach which postulates that all parties must come away having gained something—is based on a simple but important premise that involves empathy: *Negotiation takes place between human beings. You cannot negotiate with a computer or a robot.*

Therefore, to negotiate successfully you must have a knowledge of people. You must have empathy. For the negotiator, the study of man is not only proper; it is essential.

In spite of its seeming complexity, human behavior is predictable and understandable. It has a discernible pattern of development and is governed by its own internal logic. To discover the predictable elements in behavior requires an intensive kind of analysis. We should begin by learning its latitudes and its elements of forces in "normal" circumstances. With these guides, we are in a position to predict a course of behavior under a given set of circumstances. We are in a position to develop empathy.

Under certain conditions, such predictions become simpler if we consider the action of individuals as members of a large group. Then we can apply the mathematical laws of probability. In any given number of tosses of a coin, the probability is that heads will come up 50% of the time and tails 50%. The greater the number of tosses, the closer the results will agree with these percentages. In dealing on an individual basis we must be careful when we generalize, but averages give us a place to start in forming our expectations.

If you know that within one month you will find yourself negotiating either with your employees or with your fellow supervisors in a meeting, how do you prepare for this face-to-face encounter? How can you foresee the strategy of the opposite side, and how can you prepare to cope with it? The answer is not a simple one. It may be summed up, however, in the phrase reminiscent of school days: *do your home work.* There are a number of life situations for which preparation is necessary; negotiation is one of these. For successful results it requires the most intensive type of long-and short-range preparation.

An important phase of preparation for negotiation is research. Research should be objective, not in the quality of the evidence that is gathered but in the attitude toward such evidence. There is a positive reason for amassing information. It develops a wealth of material in your mind so that you may take advantage of any new development in the negotiation.

To utilize the information you obtain from research, you must rely upon your general fund of knowledge and experience. It is essential to examine a person's past history, inquire into previous transactions he was connected with, and look into every business venture or deal he has consummated. Also investigate any deals he has failed to conclude successfully. Frequently, you will learn as much, or more, about people from their failures as from their successes. If you carefully analyze the reasons that a certain deal fell through or negotiation failed, you will probably acquire a good understanding of how the other person thinks, his methods of operating, and his psychological approach. All this will give you clues to his needs and will prepare you to negotiate with him more advantageously. Consider what proposal he has made, what counter-proposals he has rejected and why, how flexible he was in the bargaining, and how emotional his approach was.

Negotiations are successful only to one who achieves the better part of his objectives regardless of the extent to which others obtain their own objectives. Only successful negotiations beget further negotiational efforts. In negotiating, you are not confined to the objectives on the agenda; sometimes discussions generate other objectives.

The subject matter is a continuing process. For this reason, it is better to take the defeat now than to argue endlessly on a subject. The continuing process of negotiations will allow us to overcome the form of a "victory" or "defeat" experienced in negotiations at a specific point in time.

Negotiations are goal-oriented "political" tools requiring extensive preparations and rehearsals for use. You must know your objectives--put them on paper. Place a minimum and maximum value on items of negotiation. You must know who the other side is.

A negotiations team should be composed only of persons who have specific functions; rules of speech and conduct should be more authoritarian than democratic. You and your fellow negotiators are not negotiators *per se* but human beings with specific circumstances and experiences.

Each negotiator inevitably has but limited authority due to variables over which he has no control regardless of his position and power. However, you should make every effort to deal with the person or persons who have the final decision and not just the intermediaries.

All elements of negotiations should be subject to control. You must do this by neutralizing all possible opponent issues. You must direct his motivations and divert his focus; you must neutralize his antagonisms; you must be conscious of what is being brought out in the opponent; and you must recognize lack of unity on the negotiating team. Compel the negotiator to identify and acknowledge the price of a negotiations breakdown to his side, and compel him to minimize the price of his "concessions" to you.

Instead of taking all you can, activate benefits for your side by what you yield to the other side. The outcome of the negotiations should be so that "winners" and "losers" alike can benefit from new decision patterns and new activities. The process of negotiations should be subject to close measurements from start to finish.

9

*Making Employee
Discipline a Positive
and Painless Matter*

As managers, we must recognize the fact that there will come the time when we must take disciplinary action. There will be times on occasion when an employee will commit an infraction of the company rules or policy. Company rules and regulations assure fair and equitable treatment for all employees. There are few, if any, employees who fail to recognize this need. To make our jobs as supervisors easier, it is necessary to use people-empathy when applying discipline. When we speak of discipline, we are talking about the necessary action that a supervisor must take as a result of a violation of company rules and regulations.

WHY A TEMPER TANTRUM IS NOT
DISCIPLINE WITH EMPATHY

In many instances when discipline is required, the supervisor closest to the situation has probably become angry. Any action requiring discipline is probably serious enough to have caused a major inconvenience (if we are lucky) or an injustice to fellow workers. It is only natural that we react to such a grave situation with emotion. Therefore, it is easy for us mentally to say, "I'll show that so-and-so!" Anger is a natural human reaction and we are not going to say that it should be suppressed. On the other hand, it must not be directed at the target of our wrath in all its untempered fury.

When we as managers use people-empathy, we know that any strong emotion, such as anger, can make it difficult for us to act in a rational and fair manner. When we are "hot under the collar," we do not think about what must be done to set the situation right; we think about extracting retribution from the offending party. Sometimes cartoons have given us the impression of the old "bull-of-the-woods" foreman steaming under the collar while firing some unlucky soul. Company policy may not allow us to take such drastic action, but we do lash out at the employee with every bit of power we can obtain within the limits of policy. If we think about this type of hostile reaction and compare it to the activities of our children, we are surprised by how closely it compares to a temper tantrum.

In many respects, when we take this type of action while under the influence of strong emotion, it is a temper tantrum. Something has gone wrong and it displeases or frustrates us, so we react in an angry manner. We feel we must do something to release this anger. A sudden burst of fury seems to be the course we might follow. If we are to manage with people-empathy so as to make our supervision easier, then we must overcome the tendency of acting when we are angry. We must find alternative ways of purging ourselves of this anger so that we might apply discipline with people-empathy. To help us manage with people-empathy, there are several principles we can follow to avoid applying punitive action that is the result of a temper tantrum:

1. Recognize that anger is a natural human emotion to which we are all subject.

2. Let the anger be expressed in a socially acceptable manner, but not in the form of disciplinary action.
3. Participate in some activity that will allow the anger to subside.
4. Talk to someone within whom you can confide, preferably your supervisor—he will have to be told of the disciplinary action sooner or later.

People-empathy helps us realize that anger is not unusual. Anger is a natural human reaction. We can expect anger to manifest itself in us from time to time. In our positions as managers, our anger is the result of some form of frustration because something happened that displeased us—especially if we felt the action that triggered our anger should not have happened. At this point, people-empathy helps us realize that we must be careful that we do not direct the manifestations of our anger at the offending party, particularly in reference to disciplinary action. However, people-empathy does not tell us *not* to get angry, but we do want to know *why* we are angry. We must seek out the source of our anger if we are to handle it. If we manage with people-empathy, we want to control our anger. By recognizing anger as a natural human emotion, we are well on our way to avoiding temper tantrums.

Once we recognize that we are angry, we need to vent this anger in a socially acceptable manner. By doing this, we are recognizing that we are experiencing a natural human emotion. We also clear the air without taking action that is vengeful. This can be accomplished by stating that we are angry and explaining the reason, by acknowledging our anger to the offending employee and explaining that we will need to think the matter over and we will be back in touch with him. If people-empathy is to make our supervision painless, however, we must not let our anger develop into disciplinary action. At this point, anger still clouds our sensibilities, and our thought processes are not conducive to fair and equitable treatment. We should be satisfied with a simple acknowledgement of the fact that we are angry.

Before acting, we must participate in some activity that will allow our anger to subside. There are a number of things we can do to relieve the tension. We can go into our office, close the door, and say what we feel in whatever words we choose—to ourselves. We might want to step outside and get a breath of fresh air. Some people find that counting helps, or going for a cup of coffee can be relaxing. At any rate, people-empathy tells us that now is not the time to act. In some instances, it might be best to let the matter rest until tomorrow. Also, in managing with people-empathy, we know that we will not have accomplished anything if we brood over the issue and think of the most drastic action we can take. Rather, we should be using this time to bring our thoughts back under control so that we can take rational action. It might even be best if we could forget about it for a little while.

By talking to someone, we can get the opinion of a person who is not immediately emotionally involved. People can react with sympathy or even empathy, but since the action did not happen to them, they will be better able to control their emotions. Rare is the company in which a supervisor can mete out immediate discipline that is arbitrary and capricious. There are usually policies that must be followed and this usually consists of steps and involves others. We must talk to our supervisor sooner or later, even if just to keep him informed. More than likely, he will have to be part of the approval process. Therefore, this would be a good opportunity to benefit from his experience. He has probably been through similar situations. By not being immediately emotionally involved, he can judge our thinking clearly and let us know if we are on the right path. Our supervisor will be more than happy to help us reach the right decision for the action we will take in an issue this important.

The complexities of human emotion show us that discipline must be handled with people-empathy if our job is to become easier. We can readily see that without people-empathy, we could easily overdo disciplinary action. We may even go so far as to take action that we could regret in the future. Managing with people-empathy gives us the tools we need to make discipline painless.

HOW BOBBY L. OVERCAME HIS TEMPER
AND MADE HIS JOB EASIER

Bobby L. was the manager of the printing room of a large newspaper. Bobby had worked his way up from printer to shift foreman to printing room manager. He was considered to be one of the true experts in the field of newspaper printing. He was also a perfectionist.

Whenever a mistake was made in "his" printing room, he blew his top. He would usually by-pass his shift foremen and go right to the guilty party. Since his temper had a short fuse, he would begin to attack the worker verbally. He would finish by suspending the employee for some period of time depending on the seriousness of the offense and how angry it made him.

The publisher was a manager who operated with people-empathy. He saw the problems that were arising in the printing room as a result of Bobby's temper tantrums. He talked with him and explained his version of the four principles of avoiding the exercise of discipline from a temper tantrum. He asked Bobby to try it over the next few days.

To Bobby's surprise, people-empathy did help make his job easier. Because everyone was no longer living in fear of his temper tantrums, they could relax and do a better job. As a result, the publisher promoted Bobby to the position of printing manager over his entire chain of newspapers.

HOW EMPATHY CAN HELP A SUPERVISOR
MAKE DISCIPLINE MOTIVATIONAL

When discipline is applied, it is usually directed to the objective of changing some form of behavior in our employees.

Whatever has happened has indicated to us a need for adjustment in behavior. It must also be done in a manner that will reinforce itself. We are changing behavioral patterns to conform to the rules and regulations of the company, or to encourage the employee to pay attention to his job to avoid costly errors and waste. In order for the discipline to be reinforcing in nature, we have felt that it must be such that it will leave an impression. In most instances, discipline is punitive in nature. This probably originated many years ago as an offshoot of our civil punitive system; it is supposed to have the same effect as spanking a child. However, this is looking at discipline from a negative point of view. We are reinforcing in the minds of our employees that they should *not* do that action again or else they will be punished again.

If we are managers who use people-empathy to make our jobs easier, we will probably find it a rare occasion when discipline is necessary. However, we are dealing with human nature which can be influenced by many things. The situation will arise when some employee will break a rule, will become careless, will show lack of effort, or any number of things warranting attention. It is then that we must handle the problem with people-empathy. In applying discipline with people-empathy, there are steps which we should follow:

1. Try to find out why the employee acted (or continues to act) as he did.
2. Find out what it will take to remove the reason for this behavior.
3. Find positive (rather than punitive) ways of encouraging improvement in behavior.

We can establish a general rule that most employees are not deliberate rule breakers. For the most part, employees will try to live within the system of rules and procedures or work to change them if they feel there is a need for change. Therefore, when an employee does something that is contrary to the norm, there must be a reason for it. It is when an employee acts in such a manner that we get our clue that something is wrong. When we manage with people-empathy, we recognize this fact and begin looking for the source of the problem. Suppose an employee becomes a chronic tardiness problem; we should investigate to find out why. There has to be a reason for this employee's tardiness, particularly if he had no problems previously. This is an important aspect of managing with people-empathy. Also, we can see why we must allow our anger to subside before proceeding. It is not enough to come down hard on the tardiness; rather, we must seek out the source of the problem and help the employee resolve it, and then we can expect the problem to cease.

Once we have found the reason for our employee acting in an unacceptable manner, we must then find a way of removing it. We must be able to do this in a calm, rational manner. In most cases, adverse behavior is a symptom of other problems. When an employee does things that would be cause for discipline, it is usually the result of some hidden difficulty. Therefore, these problems must be removed before we can expect a change in behavior. When we manage with people-empathy we look for these reasons. If we are to be effective managers, we must make every effort to find out what is causing this behavior so that we can help our employee. These problems can take many forms such as personal illness, financial difficulties, home worries, boredom with the present job, an excessive amount of overtime, and so on. The problem can even be with ourselves as managers. Until we find it, though, we are not in a position to help. In using people-empathy to help remove the problem we realize that we must be careful that we don't violate an employee's right to privacy. In other words, if the employee is having marital difficulties, we must not be interested in a blow-by-blow account.

If we have an employee who is plagued with financial difficulties and we suspend him for a few days without pay, we are only compounding his problem. That is why we must use

people-empathy to make discipline positive rather than punitive. The action we take must be appropriate to the situation
and must be beneficial. It must be directed toward a change in
behavior. When we use people-empathy, we are limited only by
our imagination. We can use personal counseling techniques, set
up special training sessions, put the employee in contact with
professionals who can help overcome problems of special
nature, buy the employee an alarm clock, develop special job
assignments that will relieve boredom, and use the principles of
motivation discussed in earlier chapters. If we can't think of the
appropriate action that would help, we should seek assistance.
The personnel department would be a good place to start.
Punitive action should be reserved as a last resort when all else
fails. However, if we find that we have done everything we can
within our scope to help the employee and the problem persists,
then, and only then is punitive action required. The best thing
for both the employee and you by this time would be a mutual
agreement for termination. People-empathy will help us realize
that this is in the best interest of both parties. However, if we
use people-empathy in applying discipline, we will be able to
make it motivational.

HOW MARY G. TURNED A PROBLEM
EMPLOYEE INTO A PERFORMER AND
EARNED AN EXTRA MONTH'S SALARY

As Employee Relations Coordinator for a large automotive
supply company, Mary G. had a staff of six employees working
for her. When Mary took over the department, her supervisor
warned her about one of the employees. It seemed that this
particular employee was a chronic problem, but he knew where
the limits were and always managed to stay out of reach of
being terminated.

Mary used people-empathy as a manager. She began examin-
ing the situation involving this employee. Mary was looking for
the problem that was causing this employee to act as he did.

After looking at the symptoms and several counseling sessions, she found that this employee was essentially bored with his job. He was a smart employee whose job was so routine that it left him no challenge. Mary began working on enriching this employee's job. She also put him in charge of several important projects.

The employee who was a chronic problem became a real performer for his company. Mary's department increased its productivity and efficiency so much that she, and everyone in her department, received a year-end bonus equal to one month's salary.

WHAT THE SUPERVISOR SHOULD
ACCOMPLISH WITH DISCIPLINE THROUGH
EMPATHY

When we hear the word "discipline" we often think of punishment. It has been used for so many years in this manner that we have become conditioned to accept it as such. However, when we manage with people-empathy, we think of training and development. Training and development are excellent means of changing behavior—and they are painless too. Discipline, like people-empathy, is a means to an end and not an end in itself; it becomes a tool for us to use. Therefore, a supervisor should be using discipline to train and develop his employees rather than resorting to the "last resort" of punitive measures. In this way we can help our employees through positive rather than negative means. Managing with people-empathy makes this easy for us.

When we manage with people-empathy, we look for new and innovative ways to provide effective training for our employees. We are looking for the most effective and efficient means of changing behavior. This can be training that is ongoing for all employees or that provides an indoctrination for a new employee. Many times we overlook the fact that the training we used in indoctrinating our employees can be an effective source for retraining when we have a problem. It is sort of like getting back to the basics. Training need not involve expensive gadgetry, but should use the resources of our imagination. This training should serve the purpose of providing our employees with the knowledge they need in order to do the best job possible consistent with our goals and objectives. But we need not rely on a set course or seminar because it is convenient and the brochure happened to come across our desk at the right time. When we manage with people-empathy, we recognize the need in our employees for a particular type of training and then we provide it.

Discipline should also provide our employees a means of development. Training allows our employees to achieve the skills necessary for their current job. Development helps them move forward to bigger and better things. If we use development with people-empathy, then we make our jobs as supervisors much easier. Employees who are developing have no need to create problems in behavior; they are busily involved in the activities needed to produce the desired growth. Of course, this is allowing for an occasional "off day." For the most part, however, our employees will be interested in their job and in doing it to the best of their ability. We will have provided the needed stimulus to move an employee with a problem into the position of an employee who is moving ahead and being productive in the course.

Therefore, if we are providing discipline with people-empathy, we should be providing ourselves, as supervisors, more opportunity to accomplish the things that really require our attention. Actually, it can require less of our time to work with training and developing an employee than it does to apply discipline. We are not constantly burdened with decisions concerning how best to handle a problem employee. We do not have to "watch over" the employee to see if he is still acting in an adverse manner. We are not caught up in the endless details of grievance procedures or unfair labor practices. Discipline through people-empathy allows us to be supervisors.

HOW PHIL M. PREVENTED A "WAR"
BETWEEN DEPARTMENTS

When Phil M. took over as manager of the accounting department of a large company that distributes religious books and articles, it didn't take long to realize that he had a problem. One of his clerks constantly came to work late, overstayed breaks, and at times would leave work early. This was one part of the problem. Additionally, she would antagonize the workers in the EDP department. The accounting department constantly depended on the EDP department for preparation of most of its records. If any of these records were not ready when this clerk felt they should be, she would start a fuss with the keypunch operators.

It wasn't long before the keypunch operators would do what they could to keep from cooperating with her. They complained to their boss because they could not get the same preferential treatment, like coming in late in the morning.

Phil M. quickly diagnosed his problem. Being a manager who used people-empathy, he began looking for the source of the problem. In discussion with the clerk, he found that she was having trouble with her teen-age son. By offering her the name of a trained counselor and the time to meet with him, it wasn't long before the clerk became his best employee. Relations with the EDP department greatly improved, and efficiency improved in Phil's department so much that he was promoted to the position of controller.

HOW SUPERVISORS CAN ACT WITHOUT FEAR

Every once and a while, a supervisor comes along who likes to impress everyone with his authority. This can be described as the "bully approach" to management. However, most managers would rather act in accordance with the true scope of their authority, especially regarding discipline. Managers are usually aware of the fact that they cannot operate within a vacuum. This means that we cannot isolate ourselves and take action based on how we feel without involving others. When we as managers use people-empathy, we know that we must act in a manner that will keep us responsible to others. This means communicating completely with our boss. With people-empathy, we know that our supervisor is more than willing to help us. It also means involving those departments capable of working with us and advising us, such as the personnel department.

This involvement of others is essential to managing with people-empathy because it ensures fair and equitable treatment for all employees in accordance with company policies. It is certain that we do not want to act in an inconsistent manner since this only alienates employees. If we are unsure of ourselves and afraid to involve others for fear of being wrong, then this is exactly the time we need to talk to someone who can help us. When we manage with people-empathy, we know that we must do the right thing, especially regarding discipline.

Many times we have heard the phrase, "getting our ducks in a row." When we manage with people-empathy, our task becomes much easier when we "get our ducks in a row." We can act without fear when we have all the facts and have obtained sufficient inputs to enable us to take appropriate action. When we get our facts lined up, we may find that things are not as bad as they seem. With people-empathy, we know that when we have researched the situation, we are in a good position to make a fair and equitable application of company policy.

Another point that we can use with people-empathy and which should not be ignored is that we must act with consistency. This is necessary when we act with people-empathy so that our employees will know where we stand. An employee must feel that he is getting the same treatment as those before him did, and as those after him will get. When we act with people-empathy, we do not use favoritism when we are concerned with discipline. Often it is not acting with favoritism that concerns us, but rather it is acting more strictly with problem employees. This is a real problem and it takes strong effort and people-empathy to avoid it. As long as we act with consistency, we increase our opportunity of acting without fear.

A final area of consideration is knowledge of company policy. It is easy for us to fall into the trap of "thinking" we know what the policy is; however, if we manage with people-empathy and we want to make our jobs easier, we will go to the source documents that tell us what the policy is. Sometimes when source documents are written, the writer had specific objectives in mind. It might be difficult for us to understand the meaning of some policies. Therefore, we may need to consult with the company authorities on the policies. But this is what people-empathy is all about—going that extra step to make sure that our employees are treated fairly.

HOW CHARLES C. HELPED HIS COMPANY OVERCOME AN UNFAIR LABOR PRACTICE

Charles C. took over as floor superintendent at a tomato cannery when his predecessor resigned and left town. Charles was not faced with the best of situations. One of the employees had charged the former superintendent with an unfair labor practice. He claimed that he was being persecuted because he was a known union organizer. The company had clearly labeled this employee as a troublemaker.

Charles was a manager who used people-empathy. He began applying positive discipline to this employee. During the course of several training sessions, it became clear that the employee was highly skilled. As a matter of fact, he probably knew more than most foremen. It was evident that he was bored.

Charles promoted this employee to the position of process specialist. In this position, he had responsibility to troubleshoot all the lines and make sure the most efficient process was being used or to see what changes were necessary to provide top quality. The employee became so involved that he dropped his unfair labor charge. The results of creating this position of process specialist caused the company to realize a $300,000 savings due to greater process efficiencies. Charles received a substantial bonus, and a year later he was promoted to vice-president of manufacturing.

10

*How to Use People-Empathy
to Handle Tough
Supervisory Situations*

As managers, we are sometimes called upon to handle tough situations. These are the situations that do not conform to the standard "textbook" approach to management. To successfully cope with these situations we must manage with people-empathy. Management with people-empathy under these circumstances will go a long way toward making supervision painless.

HOW EMPATHY MAKES EMERGENCY
SITUATIONS EASIER TO HANDLE

Any company or business encounters emergencies of various sorts at some time or another. These emergencies can be simple in nature such as a machine breakdown, or they can be as complex as a disaster. Fortunately, not many situations fall into this latter category.

The emergencies that most of us confront are really critical situations. We are brought into the act when a problem turns messy and others can't handle it, so they come to us. This is the time that people-empathy is really going to help us. We must realize that those involved have tried some actions and failed; they are usually confused and probably frustrated.

We should use these situations as opportunities to train those who report to us. This should be done with people-empathy. In this case we should lead our employees along. With people-empathy, we must walk the fine line between doing it ourselves and letting our employees down when they are in over their head. To help our employees with people-empathy, there are several steps we should follow:

1. Help our employees re-establish effective communications.
2. Help our employees break the situation down into the contributing elements.
3. Help our employees find *the* critical situation.
4. Beginning at *the* critical situation, help our employees to determine the remedial action needed.
5. Help our employees establish priorities on the action to be taken.

Anytime a crisis occurs, communications become jumbled and a lot of misinformation appears. When we manage with people-empathy, we realize that conflict in information is probably confusing our employees. Therefore, we must take the time to help our employees re-establish effective communications. We must work with them to help them get sound, reliable information. This information will be needed before we can work out a solution to the problem.

Once we have sorted out communications, we must use this information to help our employees break down the situation into its elements. By using people-empathy, we can guide our employees through the phases of the situation that contributed to the problem. We realize that by taking the problem on in all of its glory, it can be more than we can handle. Therefore, we want to help our employees chop the situation into bite-size chunks. At the same time, we should use this opportunity to review the problem with our employees, one step at a time.

In every problem there is one element we can call *the* critical situation; that is, it is the one key element around which all other elements hinge. When we manage with people-empathy, we know that it is essential that we help our employees learn how to find this key element, or critical situation, in each problem. Once we have done this, we have provided the means to our employees for solving the problem and finding a solution.

When we have arrived at *the* critical situation, we can look for solutions. These solutions will often be a series of actions that will ultimately right the situation. Now we must use people-empathy to help our employees put the appropriate priorities on these actions. In some instances, the priorities will be fairly obvious; in other cases, it will be difficult to decide what comes first. By using our experience, we can help our employees make the right decision.

If we use people-empathy and apply these steps when possible in times of crisis when our employees need help, we can diminish the number of "emergencies." Our employees will become more self-sufficient. It will also provide them the means of coping with these situations during those times when we might not be there to help.

HOW PAUL L. FACED A CRISIS WITH
EMPATHY AND CAME THROUGH WITH EASE

Paul L. was the manager of maintenance for a local light and power company. In this position, he was responsible for three shift supervisors who, along with their crews, took care of repairs and maintenance of the lines. He also had one crew that looked after the sub-stations.

Whenever problems arose, Paul expected his supervisors to work out the difficulty and report to him as soon as they could spare their attention. However, there was one supervisor who came to Paul as soon as the situation proved to be the least bit sticky.

Paul managed with people-empathy. He realized that this supervisor was not progressing as long as Paul was handling situations for him. He also realized that his time and attention were being taken away from other areas. So Paul decided to sit down with his employee and follow the steps of handling emergency situations with people-empathy.

Paul found that it took approximately eight months to train this supervisor to handle problem situations. However, he knew that every minute would be worth it. Using people-empathy paid off. The efficiency that this supervisor attained was quite high and was seen by all. Paul realized a substantial year-end bonus and at the end of the next year, he was promoted to general manager of the light and power company.

HOW PEOPLE-EMPATHY HELPS YOU COPE WITH THE PROBLEM EMPLOYEE

Every supervisor is sure that he has at least one problem employee. Sometimes, the situation is such that the supervisor does not really have a problem employee as much as he has difficulty recognizing what motivates an employee. However, there are problem employees who do exist. There are enough in most work forces to warrant our attention.

The supervisor can usually spot a true problem employee as being a person who manifests some or all of the following traits: the employee is sure that the supervisor is showing constant favoritism; he is sure that the supervisor is withholding promotions from him; he is constantly suspicious of the motives of his fellow workers, the company, and the supervisor in particular; he is given to worries that have no truth or basis in fact; he is always dissatisfied with any and all situations; he sometimes is easily fatigued; he reacts in ways which seem to indicate that he wants the supervisor to take some sort of action against him; he sometimes "baits" a supervisor by going right up to that thin line but never crossing it; he may have trouble with drinking; he may be generally insubordinate; and in some instances, he may have displays of temper tantrums. Handling this type of employee definitely requires a substantial amount of people-empathy.

The first step in applying people-empathy to the problem employee is to be able to recognize those signs that indicate that there may be trouble. There are several specific symptoms that a supervisor can use to recognize problems before they get too far along. It is important to observe that people-empathy means that we proceed with caution and that we do *not* go on a "witch hunt." We must sensibly apply the following symptoms to those employees to whom they need be applied:

1. *Rapid changes in behavior.* There is an old saying that "a leopard does not change its spots." For the most part, man does not change his behavior—at least not radically without some outside force stimulating this change. If an employee is normally friendly to everyone and has a "hello, have a good day" attitude and he suddenly changes to a very quiet withdrawn individual, then we know that something might be the matter.

2. *Feeling that everyone is against him.* Most employees at one time or another will feel that their luck may be down a little bit or someone has taken advantage of them. However, it is not normal for an employee to feel that everyone is taking advantage of him and that they are all "against him."

3. *Frequent displays of temper and irritation.* Most employees have their limits beyond which they will become irritated with us or at times even show hostility and temper. However, for the majority of the employees

this point is somewhere down the road. When an employee suddenly becomes irritated at the slightest whim and is constantly having one temper tantrum after another, then we can be assured that something is wrong and bothering him.

4. *Constant daydreaming.* When an employee seems to be constantly preoccupied and unable to concentrate on his chores or the instructions being given him by his supervisors or fellow workers, then there may be reason to suspect he has problems. We are all given to occasional attacks of "daydreaming," but the employee who has a problem may be constantly worrying about it to the extent that it is consuming all of his attention.

5. *Increased absenteeism and tardiness.* When an employee who is normally quite punctual and (except for a few minor illnesses) is on the job almost every day of the year suddenly starts staying out of work and coming in late, there is an indication that something is wrong. This falls into the same category as the change in the employee's outward behavior.

6. *Drinking.* Even if we do not have reason to believe that an employee is drinking on the job, if we suspect that he is doing a lot of unusually heavy drinking after his shift is over, we may have cause to suspect that we have a problem employee. We may be alerted by the fact that the employee's breath constantly smells like a hangover. If we have a reliable source of information that indicates the employee is drinking heavily, then we may have sufficient reason to believe that we have difficulties.

In handling the employee categorized as a "problem–employee" we must use people-empathy. The first thing that people-empathy tells us is that we are not experts, or professionals, in handling such an employee. If the situation warrants, we must be ready to provide professional guidance by recommending this course of action to the employee. At no time must we take the step on our own to try to provide such services as psychological counseling. As managers who use people-empathy, we should be ready to counsel with an employee using these basic principles:

1. We must pick a time when we ourselves are fairly well rested and are not pressed by other urgent items of business.
2. We must pick a place where we will not be disturbed by outside influences such as the telephone, visitors or noises.
3. We should research into the employee's background as much as possible. We should know as much as can be obtained from personnel records about the employee and his family, his likes and dislikes, his hobbies, his educational background, and such things as the part of the country in which he grew up.
4. When we sit down with the employee, we must be prepared to give him our complete and undivided attention. We must listen carefully to what he is saying.
5. We should ask the types of questions that will clarify the points being made by the employee or that will lead him along into further discussion. We should avoid asking any types of questions which the employee could construe as an invasion of privacy.
6. We should avoid offering advice during the first session, but should use the opportunity between intervening sessions to obtain advice from agencies that can provide help in these areas. This might include discussions with the personnel department.
7. We should monitor the atmosphere throughout the discussion. At no time should we let the employee engage us in arguments; and if the employee is becoming quite heated, we may want to choose to break the conversation off at this point and conclude at a later session.

8. We should avoid comment on our own part as much as possible.
9. We should take the opportunity to combine what we have learned from our research into his background with what he is saying to help us formulate opinions.
10. We must be sure to schedule further counseling sessions with the employee. We should make sure that the employee gets the feeling that we are *sincerely* interested in him. Keeping the counseling sessions long enough for the employee to unburden himself of this problem yet short enough not to wear the situation out can make these sessions more effective.

Each of these steps is designed to help us manage with people-empathy. By using people-empathy with the problem employee, we make our jobs as managers that much easier. People-empathy helps us to help the employee and at the same time to relieve ourselves of considerable burdens that can create anxieties of our own. People-empathy is not a means of escaping reality, but a means of coping with it. The problem employee can require a lot more of our attention than the other employees, but with people-empathy we must be ready to give of this time in order to help the problem employee become a productive worker.

DAVID E. EASES A TENSE SITUATION WITH EMPATHY

David E. was general manager of a computer service bureau that leased computer time to customers who did not have their own computers. Working under him were several systems analysts, computer programmers, computer operators, and key punch personnel. Not long after David took over his position, he realized that he had a real problem employee on his hands.

This employee seemed to be a maverick in the strictest sense of the word. To make matters worse, he was one of the best computer operators David had seen in a long time.

David decided that the use of people-empathy was in order. He talked to one of his supervisors in whom he could confide and found out that this employee had not always acted this way. It seemed like a change came over this employee who used to be quiet and reserved. David then began mapping out a plan of action.

Early the next day, David had a meeting with the employee. It was not the usual type of meeting where he met in his office across his desk; rather he took him down to the company canteen for a cup of coffee. After a few casual comments about the weather, David began asking him a few things about his background. He did not go into intimate detail but asked general, probing questions that would give him a basic insight into his makeup. That was about as far as he took it on that particular day.

The next day he again had coffee with this individual. After the first tidbits of conversation, David became silent. At first, the employee became silent also; then it was obvious that he was uncomfortable. Then he began talking. After listening to the employee for awhile, he began getting insight into some of the problems that were causing the employee to act this way.

David was then in the position to see the problem as the employee saw it. Over the next few weeks he began helping the employee see the solution to his problem. As a result of working with empathy, David helped this employee become the outstanding person that he was capable of being.

The results were outstanding. The increase in productivity of this employee alone, as a result of the help David gave him, was so outstanding that David's computer company was able to work out several difficult problems. As a result, David's company was awarded several top-grade contracts. At the end of the year David was awarded a sizable bonus for his efforts.

HOW EMPATHY HELPS YOU BUILD
CREDIBILITY WITH ETHNIC GROUPS

One of the toughest problems facing a supervisor today is dealing with ethnic groups. This problem definitely requires the use of people-empathy to help make supervision easier. In the real world of today, most managers do not come from ethnic or minority groups. For the purpose of our discussion here, ethnic groups and minority groups will be considered as one and the same.

The problems in dealing with ethnic groups arise out of inabilities to communicate effectively rather than problems dealing with motivation. A manager who is faced with this type of situation must seek out ways that will help him communicate with such employees.

As with any group of employees, ethnic groups also have their informal leaders. This person is usually a natural leader with whom all other members of the race or cultural background seek to identify. He is the one to whom the others bring their problems, and he is usually the one who is selected to represent the group to management. He will usually be a person with an outgoing personality.

In order to manage with people-empathy, we must work with this employee to communicate with the rest of the group. We must learn as much as we can about the background of this individual, which involves extra effort in understanding the elements that have affected his life. This extra effort is required because in most cases, we will have no experiences that qualify us to understand the background of the ethnic group involved. After we have gained the confidence of this leader, he or she can help us come to a better understanding of the group so that we can effectively communicate.

In dealing with ethnic groups, we should follow several principles if we are to be effective:

1. First and foremost, we must neither look down upon

the group nor must we react to them in a condescending manner.

2. We must make every effort to communicate with them in a manner which they can understand.

3. We must apply the same principles of motivation toward ethnic groups as we would toward any other employee.

4. We must be willing to help these employees adapt to an environment which may be totally unfamiliar to them.

5. We must consider ethnic groups as part of the entire work force and not as a work force in itself.

Most human beings do not like being treated as inferior. By looking down on any employee, we immediately cast him in the role of being inferior. By the same token, if we react to an employee in a condescending manner, we give him the impression that we honestly feel he is inferior but must treat him as we do because of rules or laws. When we hire a member of an ethnic group, we must treat him as an equal person to our other employees. This does not necessarily mean that he is equal in ability or that he has the same training and background. We may have to spend a little extra time training him in the skills required. By the same token, not every employee is endowed with the same degree of skill, but they are endowed with the same elementary makeup and do not wish to be treated as being something less than employees.

When we manage with people-empathy, we know that there are certain principles of motivation for our employees. These principles are more related to human nature than they are to a particular work activity. Therefore, we must apply these same principles of motivation to ethnic groups as we would to all of our employees. By using people-empathy in applying these principles of motivation, we will gain the maximum effort from a truly "turned on" work force. This will be one effort that will pay off in its own rewards. A motivated employee, whether or not he is from an ethnic group, is what we desire of our work force; and ethnic groups are no different. When they are truly motivated, they will return big dividends for us.

Communications will usually be difficult due to the fact that the ethnic group may speak in a language other than our own. Through cultural background, the group may employ idioms and slang to which we are not accustomed. That is why we must use people-empathy and seek out the natural leader. But communication will be necessary if we are to lead the group to the achievement of their goals and objectives within the company.

If we are to be effective in dealing with an ethnic group, we must be careful that we do not submit to the natural urge to isolate them into a separate work force. It would seem natural to isolate an ethnic group so that we can better deal with them; however, referring back to the first principle, we can readily see that this could create a situation through which the ethnic group can be made to feel inferior. Isolation can also create a natural friction between the two work forces. Prejudices that might exist will only be heightened.

Through the use of people-empathy we recognize that an ethnic group, as well as any other group, needs a source of identity. If the identity is not found within the company structure, then they will seek it within their own group. By bringing an ethnic group together as part of the overall work force of the company, we will help them to better identify with the structure of the company itself. This will then help the ethnic group to identify with the goals and objectives of the company.

HOW ROY C. DEVELOPED A RAPPORT WITH
THE ETHNIC GROUP IN HIS DEPARTMENT
AND GAINED LOYALTY AND SUPPORT

Roy C. was a department manager for a large import firm. In his department, Roy was responsible for over 100 people.

Some of his employees came from families whose origins were the Mid-East.

Because he was a manager who used people-empathy, Roy naturally applied the principles for handling ethnic groups. Since most of the employees were born in the United States, the basic language itself was not a problem; however, Roy knew that he must make every effort to communicate because there would still be difficulties arising out of cultural differences. He sought out the natural leader, who happened to be an outstanding female employee. She had a personality which everyone enjoyed, and she was also extremely intelligent and was going to night school to work on her degree. Working with her, Roy was able to come to a good understanding of this group's background and cultural mannerisms. She helped him unlock the key to understanding.

Roy carefully applied the principles of motivation and did not isolate this group of employees from the rest of the work force.

Since Roy's department was involved with imports from the Mid-East, working with this work force through people-empathy helped him more than exceed the goals and objectives set forth for his department. Because he had the loyalty of his work force and the ethnic group that was a part of it, he was able to achieve what other department managers only dreamed of achieving. At year's end, the owner of the import company rewarded him with a $5,000 bonus.

HOW EMPATHY HELPS YOU REMOVE THE PAIN FROM MEETINGS

One of the most painful experiences for some managers is the conduct of a meeting. Most managers who have had the opportunity to advance several rungs up the ladder are not concerned with speaking in front of large groups. However, the experience of trying to bring the group to the accomplishment of the meeting's purpose can be most difficult. Unless we fill the meeting with "yes" men, there is likely to be some difference of opinion. Disagreement can be essential to helping the meeting progress by pointing out all sides of an issue, but if we let the disagreement persist too long and allow hostilities to flair, the meeting can result in accomplishing nothing. To help make the job of conducting meetings easier for us, we should use people-empathy and follow these simple principles:

1. Prepare an agenda.
2. Select a suitable meeting place.
3. Make sure all who will feel the immediate impact of any decisions arising from the meeting are invited to attend.
4. Set a time limit.
5. Prepare hand-outs.
6. If special equipment is needed, be sure it is available.

By preparing an agenda, we can accomplish a couple of things. First of all, by writing down what we hope to accomplish in the meeting and the steps to achieve our objectives we can immediately determine if a meeting is necessary. Many times we think a full-fledged meeting is necessary to accomplish certain tasks when all that might be needed is to confer with the most interested party. We must remember that in having a meeting we are tying up these people and keeping them from accomplishing other tasks. Second, an agenda provides the means for keeping the meeting on track. By having a written course that we intend for the meeting to follow, it will be easier for us to keep the meeting from wandering.

In selecting a place to hold a meeting, we must consider the number of people who will be attending. If there are but a few people participating, we might hold the meeting in our office. If there are a large number of people attending we may need a conference room to seat all the participants. We must make sure that the place where we hold the meeting not only has an ample number of chairs but also has suitable facilities for the participants to use in writing and taking notes. The meeting location should be well lit and ventilated. Although it has been suggested that an ideal meeting place would be a room with no windows, tables, chairs and with no smoking allowed, it is reasonable to assume that if we are doing a good job in leading a meeting, the participants should be relatively comfortable.

In selecting those who will participate in the meeting, we should look to all who will be immediately affected by whatever decisions come out of our meeting. We must be careful here because if we were to take this to the extreme, we could include everybody in the entire company. However, we do want to make sure that the results of the meeting will include a representative opinion. In this way, we can be sure that relative inputs have been received and those who may have to live with the decision will be a part of it. By the same token, we must be careful that we are not inviting people just for the sake of inviting them.

Some meetings do not have an impact on some people. By including those who are not impacted upon in the meeting, we will be wasting their time and not receiving any meaningful inputs that will move the meeting to the desired conclusion. Therefore, we should draw up a list of those that we expect to attend and examine the list closely to determine what input we expect from each of the participants. If we find that we are including someone "out of courtesy" and cannot really expect meaningful input, we should not feel bad about crossing his name off the list. If we feel that he ought to know the outcome of the meeting, we can send him a copy of the minutes. In this way, people-empathy helps us make our meetings successful.

One thing that many managers fail to do when calling a meeting is to set a time limit. A time limit can be the best asset that a leader of the meeting can have. When we set up our agenda, we should determine how long we expect would be reasonable for us to spend on this subject. In establishing a time limit, we should have enough flexibility so that if we realize we are about to reach a conclusion and a few extra minutes are needed, then we can have them. On the other hand, the time limit should serve as a warning that if we are not about to reach the desired conclusion at that time, then we should consider marking it off and meeting at another time. In this way we will keep from tying up a lot of people who will ultimately come out of the meeting feeling tired and frustrated. We can also make sure that we do not reach a hasty decision just because everybody is tired of meeting.

In preparing for a meeting, develop handouts for all of the participants. These handouts should include not only the agenda but also necessary information for the participants who will attend the meeting. We operate with people-empathy when we realize that a participant does not appreciate having to make a decision "cold." When he is approached with the heart of the matter for the first time in the meeting and is expected to make a decision on it, he may find it somewhat difficult. In these instances, the participant may be somewhat reluctant to render a decision.

By thoroughly developing an outline of what is expected of a participant and passing it out beforehand, we give him the opportunity for research. By giving the participant this opportunity we help him become better informed about the subject on which he is to decide. We must remember that as much as we would like to go into a meeting and come out with everyone affirming our position, we do not want this to happen if the decision would be a bad one. This is the reason for having the meeting in the first place. Therefore, in order to have the best decision possible for the company we must be sure we prepare the handouts in advance and pass them out to the participants.

One final thing we should do in preparing for a meeting is to make sure that any special equipment needed will be available. Special equipment can range from a simple black-board to elaborate audio-visual aids. In some instances we may find it necessary to illustrate our point; for this, an easel pad will sometimes serve the purpose. On an easel pad we can write out what we are trying to cover. If we have slides or transparencies, we must make sure we have a slide projector or an overhead projector. Additionally, we will need a screen or other suitable surface on which to project the image. One thing we might provide would be pencil and paper if it could be reasonably expected that the participants would not bring their own. If the meeting is going to last any length of time, we might consider having facilities such as water, coffee or soft drinks. If some of the participants happen to smoke, then ash trays will be a must. For the most part, common sense should prevail and we will usually come through in fine shape.

WHAT TOM S. DID TO MAKE HIS MEETINGS SUCCESSFUL

Tom S. was a newly appointed principal of a large municipal high school. One of his first official duties was to develop a budget for the upcoming school year. Tom felt that he should hold a meeting with those who would be involved in administering the budget.

Before calling the meeting, Tom sat down and prepared an agenda. He followed each of the principles outlined for conducting a successful meeting. The meeting place would be in the school cafeteria. Tom chose this location because it would have ample seating capacity and the tables could be used for taking notes. He had decided to invite all the department heads since they would be most immediately affected by the decisions on the budget. He prepared an outline that the meeting would follow and statements of what would be expected of participants. He distributed these to the members attending so they could be prepared in advance and limit the discussion to meaningful areas. In the handouts he pointed out that the meeting would last no longer than three hours. He made sure that a portable blackboard was brought into the room and also had easel sheets available on which to illustrate certain points.

When the participants arrived for the meeting, Tom had coffee and doughnuts available. As the meeting progressed he allowed suitable discussion to take place; however, if he felt that the discussion was moving away from the topic and not leading to any desired goal, he would politely ask if we could bring the discussion back to the matter at hand. If disagreement occurred, he made sure that the dissenting party was heard. He also took care to look out for the interests of the dissenting minority to make sure that they were not "bullied" into submission. In this way, he assured that all points were heard.

At the end of his meeting, Tom felt that he had a workable budget. As soon as possible after the meeting, he had the minutes typed up. He then distributed them to all the participants, with copies to other interested parties. In this way, the participants could review the minutes and if they disagreed with any of the contents they could make their position known to Tom. Then he drafted the budget and submitted it to the school board for approval.

The meeting was so successful that Tom had one of the best budgets in the school district for the coming year. Everyone in the school who had to operate under the budget was well satisfied and did everything possible to make sure that the budget was met. This was the outstanding result of people-empathy in holding a meeting.

11

*Establishing and
Maintaining Performance
Controls Painlessly*

Thus far, it would appear that in managing with people-empathy we should have no need for controls; however, that is not the case. As successful supervisors, we must have controls to provide us with the check points needed to tell us how well we and our employees are doing. Operation without controls would be like operating without the down-markers in football. Without the markers, the football team knows it must make the first down but it doesn't know how far it has to go to get there. Managers also know certain things must be done in order to achieve the goals of the department and the company. Without controls, however, they would not know how much further they had to go to get there.

HOW EMPLOYEES CAN VIEW PERFORMANCE APPRAISALS PAINLESSLY

One of the most effective controls that a supervisor has is the performance appraisal. Even though it is one of the most useful, it is also one of the most difficult to apply. It is not an easy task to honestly appraise the performance of an individual employee and then to sit down with him and go over his weaknesses and strengths.

As managers who use people-empathy, we recognize that performance appraisal is a golden opportunity. With people-empathy, we view the performance appraisal as more than just a "report card." If we approach performance appraisal with people-empathy, we utilize it as a means to review an employee's *strengths* as well as weaknesses. We also take the performance appraisal one step further than reporting on how "good" or "bad" the employee has been doing. We view the performance appraisal as an opportunity to help the employee exploit his own strengths. We then focus on the means for the employee to strengthen his weaknesses.

Whether the performance appraisal is done on a blank sheet of paper or an elaborate form of many pages, the principles of *good* performance appraisal with people-empathy are the same. We can establish the following concepts as principles to be followed in performance appraisals:

1. Carefully analyze the accomplishment (or lack of accomplishment) of goals and objectives that were mutually set with the employee and compare them with the standards of performance that were established at the time the goals were set.
2. Review the performance of the employee against the elements of his job description.
3. Analyze the performance of the employee against the various skills, traits and abilities that contribute to effective employee performance.
4. Give the employee an overall rating.
5. Develop a performance improvement plan.

MEASURING PERFORMANCE

At the time we sat down with our employee and developed

a set of goals and objectives for his accomplishment during the year, we also established standards of performance by which we could measure whether or not the goal or objective was successfully met. When we manage with people-empathy, we must take a look at these goals and objectives in light of the established standards of performance. In this way we are giving the employee a fair and objective measure of his overall performance. It is important in managing with people-empathy that we measure the employee against his standards of performance because these will be the same measures the employee will use in developing his own image of his performance.

In terms of absolutes, we could say that an employee either met the goal or objective or failed to meet it. However, dealing with reality, it is rare that we have an opportunity to meet absolutes. In some instances the employee will meet the standards of performance. Over this situation there can be no equivocation.

However, what about the employee who exceeds the standards of performance? In these instances if we manage with people-empathy, we must recognize this fact and let the employee know we have seen this extra measure of performance. In this way we tell the employee we see that he has exceeded his standards of performance and encourage him to continue in like manner.

On the other hand, we have instances where the employee fails to meet his standards of performance; but again, we may have degrees. The employee may have partially met his goals and objectives and should be given an indication that we recognize this. In this way, the employee can be encouraged to do better. Again we may be faced with situations in which the employee has not met the goals and objectives but the reasons are not within his ability to control. In these instances, it is important that we remove the goal and objective from the list and include it only if it will be accomplished at a later time. The important point here is that operating with people-empathy, we do not rate the employee against a goal which was impossible for him to achieve because of external activities beyond his control. For instance, we may decide that a goal given to the employee must not be accomplished at this time in light of more important activities which must be done. Therefore, with people-empathy we realize that there are no absolute pass/fail situations in real life.

Therefore, we must be careful to rate our employee accordingly so that he can see how far along he has progressed in accomplishing the goals and objectives that he participated in setting with us. This is one sure means of communicating our desire to control with people-empathy. The employee is then encouraged to strive for excellence in his performance through the administration of controls with people-empathy so that he, as well as we, realizes where he stands.

REVIEWING JOB DESCRIPTION

Most of an employee's time is not spent in the conduct of activities leading to results specified in goals and objectives. Rather, an employee will find that a good portion of his working day is spent in performing those activities specified in his job description. For this reason, if we manage with people-empathy, we find that it is highly beneficial to provide some feedback to the employee on the performance of those activities set forth in his job description. Just as we have standards of performance for the completion of goals and objectives, we also have standard of performance for the completion of activities listed in the job description.

It is true that some of these activities are continuing and therefore would have no specified date for completion, but if we manage with people-empathy, we realize that we must know whether the employee has completed the task and has done a good job leading up to its completion. If we do not have these check points, then we could have a situation similar to an employee who was in an archery contest and shot the arrow into a board then drew the target around the arrow.

It is important that we talk about those activities the employee performs in which we consider his performance to be strong, as well as those activities in which he needs further strengthening. With people-empathy, we view the situation in this manner—the employee strengthens areas that are not so strong. In this manner we avoid placing him in a pass/fail situation. In managing with people-empathy we do this, not because pass/fail presents an unpleasant situation, but that the pass/fail indication accomplishes nothing in helping the employee to grow. Our ultimate goal here is to develop a system of inputs so that the employee's performance next year will be better than his performance this year.

ANALYZING SKILLS AND ABILITIES

One of the best ways to help an employee improve his performance is to look at the skills and abilities that it takes for the performance of the job. Each employee possesses these skills and abilities to varying degrees, but we as managers have a concept of what is needed to sustain standard performance. When we manage with people-empathy, we want to zero in on the skills and abilities demonstrated by the employee. Again, we are interested in the strengths of the employee as well as his weaknesses; but in discussing the weaknesses, we should be prepared to demonstrate our point with specific examples. In managing with people-empathy, we must be sure to do this if the employee is to understand what we mean.

If we are placing the performance appraisal in a written form to be included in the personnel record of this employee, we should be careful that we express exactly what we mean in writing. In this way, five years from now a new supervisor will not misconstrue what we have said. In managing with people-empathy we do not simply say, "John Jones has a poor leadership image"; instead, we discuss what it is about Mr. Jones that is causing his image to suffer. We also discuss how we recognize this problem and what we feel would be needed for the image to improve. We should also cite specific examples readily available to us that indicated this lack of the quality under discussion. In this way, when we talk to Mr. Jones, he will be in a position to understand what we are saying to him. Furthermore, and most important, by the use of people-empathy we have given him the guidelines for improvement.

PROVIDING AN OVERALL RATING

We should strive to give our employees an overall rating. When we manage with people-empathy, we realize that this is important because it ties together what we have been saying in the various parts of the performance appraisal itself. We must be careful in providing the overall rating that we are not trying merely to rank the employees in our department or company. Ranking employee performance against other employees may not be truly indicative of overall performance itself, nor the expected performance of our employees. Again we must revert to our standards of performance. We know what must be done in order to provide a truly satisfactory performance. It is against these standards that we rank our employees through the use of people-empathy. Theoretically, it is possible for all of the employees in our department to receive an average rating, a superior rating or a less than satisfactory rating. In any case, each is measured against the expected standards of performance.

Of course, we should take into consideration the length of time the person has been on the job. A fairly new employee who has been performing for only six months could not be expected to perform at the same level as the person who has been performing the job for six years. However, in using people-empathy we should rate both employees accordingly. For the employee who has only been on board for six months, we should tell him how he is performing against the expected standards of performance of a fully trained employee doing a fully satisfactory job so that he knows how far he must go in order to get to this goal. On the other hand, we should also tell him how he has been doing in his performance in the learning aspect period of his job. We will tell the employee that he is progressing faster than expected in learning his job, but he still has much to learn in order to become a fully trained employee doing a satisfactory job. In this way, we avoid giving the employee the impression that he has already attained the level of performance desired when he is fully trained and we also avoid demoralizing him by making him feel that all his work during this learning period was unnoticed.

DEVELOPING A PERFORMANCE
IMPROVEMENT PLAN

One of the most important elements of the performance appraisal, and the appraisal is incomplete unless it is present, is the development of a performance improvement plan. As we said earlier, the objective of providing performance appraisal is to have the employee improve his performance over the next year. Now, for some this might seem unnecessary since they are already doing a fully satisfactory job and are not interested in progressing any further. However, for the aspiring as well as the satisfied employee, there is a certain amount of performance that must be improved in order to stay at least at the same level. Techniques change and improvements in job activity are inevitable. Therefore, a certain amount of improvement is needed for the level of performance to stay where it is.

In preparing a performance improvement plan, we should look at the needs of the employee and marry them with the needs of the company. When we manage with people-empathy, we recognize that an employee who needs a course in budgeting could probably benefit much more if we had an in-house course geared around budgeting methods used by our own company. Many supervisors overlook the fact that reading is an excellent opportunity to gain an education. If we were to combine a reading program with counseling from ourselves, we could usually come up with an extremely effective program for the employee to follow. One way is to have the employee read a chapter or several chapters and then to sit down with us and discuss what he has read. Sometimes the only alternative available to us for particular types of knowledge needed is attendance at external activities, which are beneficial in themselves. They not only provide the course matter itself, but they also place the employee in contact with others who are in a similar situation. This is a broadening experience that can only benefit the employee. We must use people-empathy in developing a performance improvement plan so that we will tailor the plan to the specific needs of the employee.

HOW DON C. GAVE PERFORMANCE APPRAISALS THAT HELPED IMPROVE PERFORMANCE PAINLESSLY

Don C. was recently appointed to the position of production manager in a large textile company. In this position, he had responsibility for the entire production function. Don had not been in this position long before he realized that none of the employees working under him had ever received a performance appraisal. He knew that he would need to implement an effective performance appraisal system and he decided to do it with people-empathy.

With the help of his industrial relations department, he developed a performance appraisal that would be amply suited to the needs of his department and company. Don then began to have a series of meetings with his employees to explain what he was planning to do. He carefully reviewed the principles of good performance appraisals and operating with people-empathy; he assured them that by no means would he be ranking them, but rather would be helping them to improve their performance from one year to the next. He went over the proposed program that had been previously drawn up and solicited their inputs. The employees responded well to the proposed program.

After Don had gone through two appraisal periods with his employees, he began to note a marked improvement in performance. The results of implementing a performance appraisal system with people-empathy were so spectacular that during the next year Don was promoted to general manager of the apparel division.

HOW SUCCESSFUL SUPERVISORS EMPLOY APPRAISALS

Supervisors who manage with people-empathy recognize that good performance appraisal technique deals largely with results. When managing with people-empathy, we do not deal in intangible areas. Rather, we look at the performance appraisal in terms of the goals, objectives and standards of performance previously set by the employee and his supervisor. As successful managers, we recognize that the true purpose of a performance appraisal is to help the employee improve performance. It is precisely for this reason that we must avoid dealing in the employee's personality. Rather, we are interested in helping the employee improve skills and techniques that can lead to overall performance improvement.

Managers who use people-empathy recognize that their primary emphasis should be on the picture as a whole rather than concentration on one specific incident. We must avoid the "halo" effect—that is, we should not allow a single incident in which the employee was outstanding to cloud over other instances where the employee did not do so well. When employing performance appraisal with people-empathy, we should also make sure that the time frame does not influence us. It is very easy for us to recall recent events to the exclusion of those things that occurred earlier during the rating period.

Managers who use people-empathy will take great pains and go through several steps to make sure that a performance appraisal is correct. These steps can be outlined as follows:

1. The manager should do his homework thoroughly before the performance appraisal session. He should complete a preparatory review of the record of the employee's performance over the rating term. Successful managers usually keep little notes in a central location to refresh their memories at appraisal time. The supervisor should also review the most recent previous rating given to the employee. The supervisor should do all of this at a time when he can give his full concentration without interruptions.

2. In developing the ratings, the supervisor should try to be as specific as possible. General impressions about a particular factor can only create questions in the long run. If we feel that an employee's performance is a certain way, we had to obtain this knowledge from somewhere. Therefore, we should recall as many specific incidents as possible that illustrate what we are describing.

3. We should take careful pains to rate our employee against the job requirements and the standards of performance which we set up earlier. We must avoid, at all cost, a comparative rating—that is, rating the employee against the performance of other employees.

4. We must avoid any attempts to "soften the blow" of the performance appraisal. If we feel that an employee is lacking in a certain area, we should be willing to discuss it with him. This does not mean that we have to be blunt and untactful, but it does mean that if we are managing with people-empathy we must be honest.

5. We should be sure that we are rating the employee since his last performance appraisal. Each rating period is a

"new ball game" and should not reflect a carryover from a previous rating. The previous rating period can be used as comparison to see if the employee has truly improved. But we must avoid the effect that the good and the bad from a previous period can produce if we dwell upon it too long. We must manage with people-empathy and give our employees credit for the work that they are currently doing.

If the objective of performance appraisal is performance improvement, then truly the appraisal must be a vehicle for learning. If we are to use it as such, then we must do so with people-empathy. Therefore, we must avoid giving it the aura of a "report card." We should also avoid using it as a tool for ammunition: it should not be the source for "writing the employee up." Rather, it should be a means for pointing out the weakness that the employee might have and illustrating ways in which he can improve his performance. We must also avoid using the performance appraisal as a means of getting on a soapbox and putting forth our own personal philosophies. We should stick to established management practice. When we use performance appraisals with people-empathy, the employee is then able to judge how effective or ineffective his performance has been during the past rating period. He is also able to make the appropriate adjustments to bring his performance in line with expectations.

Successful managers who use performance appraisals with people-empathy realize that the appraisal process cannot stop with a judgment about performance. Successful supervisors look for the aid in assistance that can help the employee in improving his performance. They provide their employees with many tools to help them. These tools range from on-the-job training to personal counseling, reading assignments, to formalized or specialized training. It is through people-empathy that successful supervisors employ performance appraisals.

HOW THE DRYDON COMPANY EMPLOYED ITS
APPRAISAL SYSTEM WITH EMPATHY

The Drydon Company was a small company engaged in the air transport business. Their primary business centered around carrying mail, charter flights, special cargo flights, a flight school, and the repair and maintenance of aircraft and equipment. The Drydon Company was a small company compared to many major corporations. It was also young; however, its main feature was its growth.

The president and general manager of the Drydon Company was a dynamic individual who managed with people-empathy. He realized if they were to continue growing and stay competitive, he would have to develop a program that would allow his employees to continue improvement each year. He decided that the best way to accomplish this would be through the installation of a performance appraisal program. The Drydon Company realized that there were many "canned" performance appraisal programs available. They knew that they could probably go to a local library, look in a book, pick up a program and tell their supervisors to use it. However, being a company involved with people-empathy, they realized that this type of program would have very little positive effect on the employees.

In order to have the most effective program possible, the Drydon Company began by holding several training sessions in performance appraisals. These sessions covered the background of performance appraisal, its purpose, and the qualities of a good performance appraisal that would ensure its success. The supervisors held special sessions with all employees on performance appraisals so that they would be well aware of what was happening. Then from the base of knowledge derived, all the supervisors together developed a performance appraisal program to be used by the Drydon Company that would be relevant and meaningful to its employees. The employees were also consulted on the elements included in the performance appraisal. Many suggestions which they brought up were incorporated.

The Drydon Company was then able to install a performance appraisal program sure of success. However, it didn't stop there. It continued its training program and constantly upgraded the system it was using. The first year after the installation of this program, the Drydon Company witnessed a 33% improvement in productivity. Its profits doubled and expenses were minimized.

HOW SUPERVISORS CAN VIEW BEHAVIOR
WITH EMPATHY

As managers who use people-empathy, we realize that all employees will not be motivated at the same time to the same degree. What's more, it is highly unlikely that we will have provided for all of our employees' maintenance needs. Therefore, it is essential that we use people-empathy to observe the behavior of our employees. It is this behavior that will keep us tuned in to what is happening with our employees. By viewing behavior with people-empathy, we will be able to notice possible causes of trouble and dissatisfaction before they start. We have all seen or heard from time to time that a "leopard does not change its spots." This is passed on to us as the warning sign for problems. This means that if we are tuned into our people and we notice a severe change in them, then it is entirely possible that we have a problem on our hands.

We are all generally familiar with these signs. We know that if an employee is normally outgoing and cheerful, yet for some reason or another he has been extremely sullen and withdrawn lately, we can be sure there is something wrong. Perhaps a normally "safe" employee suddenly starts having a rash of accidents. These are the symptoms that we discussed in coping with a problem employee, but behavior can be even deeper than this.

When we manage with people-empathy we are interested in subtle changes in behavior. Suppose the change has come about immediately after we have given our employee additional responsibility. We can also look for such signs as the employee turning in work that is substandard to his usual quality. In this situation we can suspect that perhaps we have thrust the employee in too deep and have not given him the means to sustain himself. Therefore, he is subtly asking us to help him.

We might be confronted with a situation in which we have placed the employee in jeopardy. Suppose through inadvertent actions on our part we have made him a fair-haired "boy wonder." Suppose for the sake of a given project we have more or less put him on an equal footing with other supervisors under us by having him report directly to us. Let us further assume that we are familiar with the overall aspects of what we expect from this employee, but our position has removed us from the intimate details that would allow us to advise this employee. As a result of this incongruous situation, we have now caused this employee embarrassment since he cannot comfortably ask his new "peers" for assistance; we are unable to give him the vital assistance he needs. Therefore, in this "sink or swim" situation that we have created, the employee can do nothing more than sink. However, if we had monitored his situation with people-empathy, we would have been aware of the monster we were creating. We would have been better prepared in the earlier stages if we put him in a situation that would provide him all the needed help to grow into his new job. It takes people-empathy to view behavior such as this; without it, we are unable to view the situation in a manner that will give us concrete feedback so that we can take positive action.

HOW TO OVERCOME DIFFICULTIES IN EMPATHY ENCOUNTERED WITH CONTROLS

In all our discussions so far, it would appear that people-empathy is not compatible with controls. As a matter of fact, we discussed how to remove controls in Chapter 5. However, some controls are essential as monitoring points throughout the operation. As we discussed in Chapter 1, supervisors still have the responsibility for the job which they are performing. Therefore, we need these controls to alert us as to the status of conditions at any given moment of time. But we must monitor and control with people-empathy.

From time to time we will encounter difficulties with controls. At times these difficulties will seem to put us at odds with what we feel is right with people-empathy. Situations such as these require careful analysis and review. At times like this, it would probably be well if we could get off to ourselves. While we are sitting and thinking about the situation, we would do well to write out a list of what we feel are key points to the problem. This list will help us avoid overlooking something important.

Once we have analyzed what we feel are the key points to the problem, then we need to look at our needs, the needs of the company and the relationship of these needs to the controls. Again we must look at the situation with people-empathy. It is at this point that we are often able to see where we have gone wrong. Perhaps we have misunderstood the needs; or again, maybe we have applied controls that weren't necessary; or perhaps the problem was not really a conflict between the controls and people-empathy but a failure to communicate. Whatever the problem is, once we have found it we are then able to correct it. Often the problem resolves itself.

Sometimes, a supervisor may find that his controls aren't working. In this instance he is left without a means of monitoring the situation. Again this is going to require analysis; only this time, if the supervisor is managing with people-empathy he will realize that he should not go off and act alone. What he really needs to do is sit down with his supervisors and key employees and analyze the situation thoroughly. Some of the processes for analysis will be the same. We must once again define our objectives and also look at the needs. When we do this, we can once again establish what types of controls are best suited to give us the information we need. Again, we must be aware of the fact that when we set controls they must be mutually agreed upon. In this way everyone will be involved and can recognize his role in making the controls work. Everyone will be aware of what is expected of him and what standards are required to meet these expectations. Through the use of people-empathy, we will be able to take positive action to correct controls that are out of order and make them more effective.

HOW THE MEETING THAT LARRY A. HAD
EARNED HIM A PROMOTION

Larry A. was a superintendent in a company that manufactured clocks and clock parts. Since he had taken over his position, his department had moved ahead with great stride. Among his superiors he was noted as being a "comer"; however, lately he had not been having his usual success. Deadlines were sometimes missed, costs were overrunning the budget, and in general it appeared that his controls were just not working.

Larry's supervisor was a manager who used people-empathy. After analyzing Larry's problem, he determined that his controls weren't completely at fault. Larry was having some difficulty in administering the controls. Apparently, Larry was on to the theme of participative management and could not seem to "marry" the concept of controls with his newly found style of management. Larry's supervisor called him in and explained to him the difference in types of management and how controls were actually compatible with managing with people-empathy. He suggested that Larry should call his supervisors together and sit down with them. At their meeting they should discuss the goals and objectives they are trying to meet and let the managers participate in establishing the controls to guide them along their route.

Larry thought about this awhile and then planned his

meeting. At first, it appeared as if the meeting was not going to be too successful. Many of those participating seemed to be using this meeting as an opportunity to air their personal gripes. Others caused the meeting to wander off in different directions. Then Larry reflected upon things that his supervisor had recently told him. He realized that if he was going to be the leader, he had to guide the meeting and keep it on course. From that point on things got better. Larry also realized that they were not going to finish in just one session. Therefore, after using this first meeting as a warm-up, they decided to allow a week for all the supervisors to research the matter and be prepared at the next meeting to get down to some hard facts and "brass tacks."

As a result of managing with people-empathy, Larry was able to re-establish controls that were extremely effective. His goals and objectives got back on course, and he made his deadlines well within the time limit and got costs well under budget. The controls were beginning to work again. As a result of his efforts to people-empathy, Larry was again recognized as a "comer" and was promoted to the position of vice president of manufacturing with an increase in salary of $5,000 a year.

ACHIEVING RESULTS WITH CONTROLS
CAN BE PAINLESS

Controls become an absolute necessity when we realize that as managers we need some system of making the entire scope of our job just a little more predictable. For this purpose, controls should apply to all of our resources, including the human resource. It is this element of human application that brings about the need for people-empathy. Of course, there are controls and *there are controls.* On one end of the spectrum would be a slave driver with a whip. On the other end of the spectrum is the "ideal" manager who controls by using nothing more than his own charisma. However, as managers who use people-empathy, we realize that one extreme is totally undesirable and the other extreme is probably unattainable.

One thing that works in our favor as managers who use people-empathy is the fact that people largely want to have some measure of control over their own actions. This desire of an employee to exercise control and our need to have controls can work together in close harmony. People-empathy helps us to understand this fact: here we are adapting to a person's needs and not bending him to do our will. People-empathy helps us to realize that controls need not be arbitrary and capricious; rather, if they are uniformly set with the participation of the employees involved, controls can be highly effective.

One of the easiest ways of setting up controls painlessly is the involvement of the employee. This is the type of involvement which we have spoken about throughout this book. What we are doing here is allowing the employees to commit themselves to the needed achievement. Applying controls with people-empathy is much more effective than our committing the employees to goals. Our commitment on behalf of the employees is hardly their commitment; besides, what we may have committed them to may be unreasonable. Also, commitment is always a two-way street. We should not only expect commitment from our employees, but we should also give our commitment to the employees to help them in achieving their goals and objectives. This is where people-empathy really helps us to succeed as managers.

Controlling is often listed as one of the functions of managing. Truly it is necessary if we are to be successful and accomplish those things that require our attention. People-empathy goes a long way in helping us manage this function called controlling. It helps us achieve the desired results painlessly.